Statistical Analysis with R Essentials

by Joseph Schmuller, PhD

Statistical Analysis with R Essentials For Dummies®

Published by: **John Wiley & Sons, Inc.**, 111 River Street, Hoboken, NJ 07030-5774, www.wiley.com

Copyright © 2024 by John Wiley & Sons, Inc., Hoboken, New Jersey

Published simultaneously in Canada

For general information on our other products and services, please contact our Customer Care Department within the U.S. at 877-762-2974, outside the U.S. at 317-572-3993, or fax 317-572-4002. For technical support, please visit https://hub.wiley.com/community/support/dummies.

Wiley publishes in a variety of print and electronic formats and by print-on-demand. Some material included with standard print versions of this book may not be included in e-books or in print-on-demand. If this book refers to media such as a CD or DVD that is not included in the version you purchased, you may download this material at http://booksupport.wiley.com. For more information about Wiley products, visit www.wiley.com.

Library of Congress Control Number: 2024933673

ISBN 978-1-394-26342-4 (pbk); ISBN 978-1-394-26344-8 (ebk); ISBN 978-1-394-26343-1 (ebk)

SKY10070014_031924

Contents at a Glance

Table of Contents

Introduction

As the title indicates, this book covers the essentials of statistics and R. Although it's designed to get you up and running in a hurry, and to quickly answer your questions, it's not just a cookbook. Before I tell you about one of R's features, I give you the statistical foundation it's based on. My goal is that you understand that feature when you use it — and that you use it effectively.

In the proper context, R can be a great tool for learning statistics and for refreshing what you already know. I've tried to supply that context in this book.

About This Book

Although the development of statistics concepts proceeds in a logical way, I organized this book so you can open it up in any chapter and start reading. The idea is for you to quickly find what you're looking for and use it immediately — whether it's a statistical concept or an R feature.

On the other hand, cover-to-cover is okay if you're so inclined. If you're a statistics newbie and you have to use R to analyze your data, I recommend you begin at the beginning.

One caveat: I don't cover R graphics. Although graphics are a key feature of R, I confined this book to statistics concepts and how R implements them.

Foolish Assumptions

I'm assuming:

>> You know how to work with Windows or the Mac. I don't go through the details of pointing, clicking, selecting, and so forth.

>> You'll be able to install R and RStudio (I show you how in Chapter 2), and follow along with the examples. I use the

Windows version of RStudio, but you should have no problem if you're working on a Mac.

Icons Used in This Book

Icons appear all over *For Dummies* books, and this one is no exception. Each one is a little picture in the margin that lets you know something special about the paragraph it's next to.

TIP

This icon points out a hint or a shortcut that helps you in your work and makes you a finer, kinder, and more insightful human being.

REMEMBER

This one points out timeless wisdom to take with you on your continuing quest for knowledge.

WARNING

Pay attention to this icon. It's a reminder to avoid something that might gum up the works for you.

Where to Go from Here

You can start the book anywhere, but here are a couple of hints. Want to learn the foundations of statistics? Turn the page. Introduce yourself to R? That's Chapter 2. For anything else, find it in the Table of Contents or in the Index and go for it.

Chapter **1**
Data, Statistics, and Decisions

S tatistics, first and foremost, is about *decision-making*. Statisticians look at data and wonder what the numbers are saying.

R helps you crunch the data and compute the numbers. As a bonus, R can also help you comprehend statistical concepts.

Developed specifically for statistical analysis, R is a computer language that implements many of the analytical tools statisticians have developed for decision-making. I wrote this book to show how to use these tools in your work.

The Statistical (and Related) Notions You Just Have to Know

The analytical tools that R provides are based on statistical concepts in the remainder of this chapter. These concepts are based on common sense.

Samples and populations

If you watch TV on election night, you know that one of the main events is the prediction of the outcome immediately after the polls close (and before all the votes are counted).

The idea is to talk to a *sample* of voters right after they vote. If they're truthful about how they marked their ballots, and if the sample is representative of the *population* of voters, analysts can use the sample data to draw conclusions about the population.

That, in a nutshell, is what statistics is all about — using the data from samples to draw conclusions about populations.

Here's another example. Imagine that your job is to find the average height of 10-year-old children in the United States. Because you probably wouldn't have the time or the resources to measure every child, you'd measure the heights of a representative sample. Then you'd average those heights and use that average as the estimate of the population average.

Estimating the population average is one kind of *inference* that statisticians make from sample data. I discuss inference in more detail in the upcoming section "Inferential Statistics: Testing Hypotheses."

REMEMBER

Here's some important terminology: Properties of a population (like the population average) are called *parameters*, and properties of a sample (like the sample average) are called *statistics*. If your only concern is the sample properties (like the heights of the children in your sample), the statistics you calculate are *descriptive*. If you're concerned about estimating the population properties, your statistics are *inferential*.

REMEMBER

Now for an important convention about notation: Statisticians use Greek letters (μ, σ, ρ) to stand for parameters, and English letters ($\bar{X}$, s, r) to stand for statistics. Figure 1-1 summarizes the relationship between populations and samples, and between parameters and statistics.

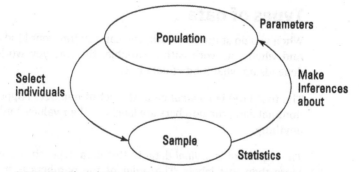

FIGURE 1-1: The relationship between populations, samples, parameters, and statistics.

Variables: Dependent and independent

A *variable* is something that can take on more than one value — like your age, the value of the dollar against another currency, or the number of games your favorite sports team wins. Something that can have only one value is a *constant*. Scientists tell us that the speed of light is a constant, and we use the constant π to calculate the area of a circle.

Statisticians work with *independent* variables and *dependent* variables. In any study or experiment, you'll find both kinds. Statisticians assess the relationship between them.

A dependent variable is what a researcher *measures*. In an experiment, an independent variable is what a researcher *manipulates*. In some contexts, a researcher can't manipulate an independent variable. Instead, he notes naturally occurring values of the independent variable and how they affect a dependent variable.

In general, the objective is to find out whether changes in a dependent variable are associated with changes in an independent variable.

In examples that appear throughout this book, I show you how to use R to calculate characteristics of groups of scores, or to compare groups of scores. Whenever I show you a group of scores, I'm talking about the values of a dependent variable.

Types of data

When you do statistical work, you can run into four kinds of data. And when you work with a variable, the way you work with it depends on what kind of data it is:

The first kind is *nominal* data. If a set of numbers happens to be nominal data, the numbers are labels — their values don't signify anything.

The next kind is *ordinal* data. In this data-type, the numbers are more than just labels. The order of the numbers is important. If I ask you to rank ten foods from the one you like best (one), to the one you like least (ten), we'd have a set of ordinal data.

But the difference between your third-favorite food and your fourth-favorite food might not be the same as the difference between your ninth-favorite and your tenth-favorite. This type of data lacks equal intervals and equal differences.

The third kind of data, *interval*, gives us equal differences. The Fahrenheit scale of temperature is a good example. The difference between 30° and 40° is the same as the difference between 90° and 100°. Each degree is an interval.

On the Fahrenheit scale, a temperature of 80° is not twice as hot as 40°. For ratio statements ("twice as much as," "half as much as") to make sense, "zero" has to mean the complete absence of the thing you're measuring. A temperature of 0°F doesn't mean the complete absence of heat — it's just an arbitrary point on the Fahrenheit scale. (The same holds true for Celsius.)

The fourth kind of data, *ratio*, provides a meaningful zero point. On the Kelvin Scale of temperature, zero means "absolute zero," where all molecular motion (the basis of heat) stops. So 200° Kelvin is twice as hot as 100° Kelvin. Another example is length. Eight inches is twice as long as four inches. "Zero inches" means "a complete absence of length."

An independent variable or a dependent variable can be either nominal, ordinal, interval, or ratio. The analytical tools you use depend on the type of data you work with.

A little probability

When statisticians make decisions, they use probability to express their confidence about those decisions. They can never be absolutely certain about what they decide. They can only tell you how *probable* their conclusions are.

What do we mean by probability? In my experience, the best way to understand probability is with examples.

If you toss a coin, what's the probability that it turns up heads? If the coin is fair, you might figure that you have a 50-50 chance of heads and a 50-50 chance of tails. And you'd be right. In terms of the kinds of numbers associated with probability, that's ½.

Think about rolling a fair die (one member of a pair of dice). What's the probability that you roll a 4? Well, a die has six faces and one of them is 4, so that's ⅙.

Still another example: Select one card at random from a standard deck of 52 cards. What's the probability that it's a diamond? A deck of cards has four suits, so that's ¼.

In general, the formula for the probability that a particular event occurs is

$$Pr(event) = \frac{\text{Number of ways the event can occur}}{\text{Total number of possible events}}$$

At the beginning of this section, I say that statisticians express their confidence about their conclusions in terms of probability, which is why I brought all this up in the first place. This line of thinking leads to *conditional* probability — the probability that an event occurs given that some other event occurs. Suppose that I roll a die, look at it (so that you don't see it), and tell you that I rolled an odd number. What's the probability that I've rolled a 5? Ordinarily, the probability of a 5 is ⅙, but "I rolled an odd number" narrows it down. That piece of information eliminates the three even numbers (2, 4, 6) as possibilities. Only the three odd numbers (1,3, 5) are possible, so the probability is ⅓.

What's the big deal about conditional probability? What role does it play in statistical analysis? Read on.

Inferential Statistics: Testing Hypotheses

Before a statistician does a study, he draws up a tentative explanation — a *hypothesis* that tells why the data might come out a certain way. After gathering all the data, the statistician has to decide whether or not to reject the hypothesis.

That decision is the answer to a conditional probability question — what's the probability of obtaining the data, given that this hypothesis is correct? Statisticians have tools that calculate the probability. If the probability turns out to be low, the statistician rejects the hypothesis.

Back to coin-tossing for an example: Imagine that you're interested in whether a particular coin is fair — whether it has an equal chance of heads or tails on any toss. Let's start with "The coin is fair" as the hypothesis.

To test the hypothesis, you'd toss the coin a number of times — let's say, a hundred. These 100 tosses are the sample data. If the coin is fair (as per the hypothesis), you'd expect 50 heads and 50 tails.

If it's 99 heads and 1 tail, you'd surely reject the fair-coin hypothesis: The conditional probability of 99 heads and 1 tail given a fair coin is very low. Of course, the coin could still be fair and you could, quite by chance, get a 99-1 split, right? Sure. You never really know. You have to gather the sample data (the 100 toss-results) and then decide. Your decision might be right, or it might not.

Null and alternative hypotheses

Think again about that coin-tossing study I just mentioned. The sample data are the results from the 100 tosses. I said that we can start with the hypothesis that the coin is fair. This starting point is called the *null hypothesis*. The statistical notation for the null hypothesis is H_0. According to this hypothesis, any heads-tails split in the data is consistent with a fair coin. Think of it as the idea that nothing in the sample data is out of the ordinary.

An alternative hypothesis is possible — that the coin isn't a fair one and it's biased to produce an unequal number of heads and tails. This hypothesis says that any heads-tails split is consistent with an unfair coin. This alternative hypothesis is called, believe it or not, the *alternative hypothesis*. The statistical notation for the alternative hypothesis is H_1.

Now toss the coin 100 times and note the number of heads and tails. If the results are something like 90 heads and 10 tails, it's a good idea to reject H_0. If the results are around 50 heads and 50 tails, don't reject H_0.

Notice that I did *not* say "accept H_0." The way the logic works, you *never* accept a hypothesis. You either reject H_0 or don't reject H_0.

REMEMBER

Two types of error

Whenever you evaluate data and decide to reject H_0 or to not reject H_0, you can never be absolutely sure. You never really know the "true" state of the world.

Because you're never certain about your decisions, you can make an error either way you decide. As I mention earlier, the coin could be fair and you just happen to get 99 heads in 100 tosses. That's not likely, and that's why you reject H_0 if that happens. It's also possible that the coin is biased, yet you just happen to toss 50 heads in 100 tosses. Again, that's not likely and you don't reject H_0 in that case.

Although those errors are not likely, they are possible. They lurk in every study that involves inferential statistics. Statisticians have named them *Type I* errors and *Type II* errors.

If you reject H_0 and you shouldn't, that's a Type I error. In the coin example, that's rejecting the hypothesis that the coin is fair, when in reality it is a fair coin.

If you don't reject H_0 and you should have, that's a Type II error. It happens if you don't reject the hypothesis that the coin is fair, and in reality it's biased.

How do you know if you've made either type of error? You don't — at least not right after you make the decision to reject or not reject H_0. (If it's possible to know, you wouldn't make the error in the first place!) All you can do is gather more data and see if the additional data is consistent with your decision.

Chapter **2**
Introducing R

R is a computer language. It's a tool for doing the computation and number-crunching that set the stage for statistical analysis and decision-making.

RStudio is an open source integrated development environment (IDE) for creating and running R code. It's available in versions for Windows, Mac, and Linux. Although you don't need an IDE in order to work with R, RStudio makes life a *lot* easier.

Downloading R and RStudio

First things first. Download R from the Comprehensive R Archive Network (CRAN). In your browser, type this address if you work in Windows:

```
cran.r-project.org/bin/windows/base/
```

Type this one if you work on the Mac:

```
cran.r-project.org/bin/macosx/
```

Click the link to download R. This puts the win.exe file in your Windows computer, or the .pkg file in your Mac. In either case, follow the usual installation procedures. When installation is complete, Windows users see an R icon on their desktop; Mac users see it in their `Applications` folder.

Both URLs provide helpful links to FAQs. The windows-related URL also links to "Installation and other instructions."

TIP

I'm using R version 4.3.2. If you use a different version of R, your code may not perform exactly as mine does, and some of your code's output may be somewhat different from mine.

TIP

Now for RStudio. Here's the URL:

```
https://posit.co/download/rstudio-desktop/
```

Click the link for the installer for your computer, and again follow the usual installation procedures.

After the RStudio installation is finished, click the RStudio icon to open the window shown in Figure 2-1.

FIGURE 2-1: RStudio, immediately after you install it.

TIP

I'm using RStudio 2023.12.1 Build 402. If you already have an older version of RStudio and you go through this installation procedure, the install updates to the latest version (and you don't have to uninstall the older version).

The large Console pane on the left runs R code. One way to run R code is to type it directly into the Console pane. I show you another way in a moment.

The other two panes provide helpful information as you work with R. The Environment and History pane is in the upper right. The Environment tab keeps track of the things you create (which R calls *objects*) as you work with R. The History tab tracks R code that you enter. Your History tab will look different from my History tab in Figure 2-1.

Get used to the word *object*. Everything in R is an object.

TIP

The Files, Plots, Packages, and Help tabs are in the pane in the lower right. The Files tab shows files you create (again, yours will look different from mine). The Plots tab holds graphs you create from your data. (I don't cover graphics in this book.) The Packages tab shows add-ons (called *packages*) you downloaded as part of the R installation. Bear in mind that "downloaded" doesn't mean "ready to use." To use a package's capabilities, one more step is necessary — and believe me, you'll want to use packages.

Figure 2-2 shows the Packages tab. The packages are in either the user library (which you can see in the figure) or the system library (which you have to scroll down to). I discuss packages later in this chapter.

Files	Plots	Packages	Help	Viewer		
Install	Update					
Name		Description			Version	
System Library						
boot		Bootstrap Functions (Originally by Angelo Canty for S)			1.3-18	
class		Functions for Classification			7.3-14	
cluster		"Finding Groups in Data": Cluster Analysis Extended Rousseeuw et al.			2.0.4	
codetools		Code Analysis Tools for R			0.2-14	
compiler		The R Compiler Package			3.3.1	
datasets		The R Datasets Package			3.3.1	
foreign		Read Data Stored by Minitab, S, SAS, SPSS, Stata, Systat, Weka, dBase, ...			0.8-66	
graphics		The R Graphics Package			3.3.1	
grDevices		The R Graphics Devices and Support for Colours and Fonts			3.3.1	
grid		The Grid Graphics Package			3.3.1	
KernSmooth		Functions for Kernel Smoothing Supporting Wand & Jones (1995)			2.23-15	
lattice		Trellis Graphics for R			0.20-33	
MASS		Support Functions and Datasets for			7.3-45	

FIGURE 2-2: The RStudio Packages tab.

The Help tab, shown in Figure 2-3, provides links to a wealth of information about R and RStudio.

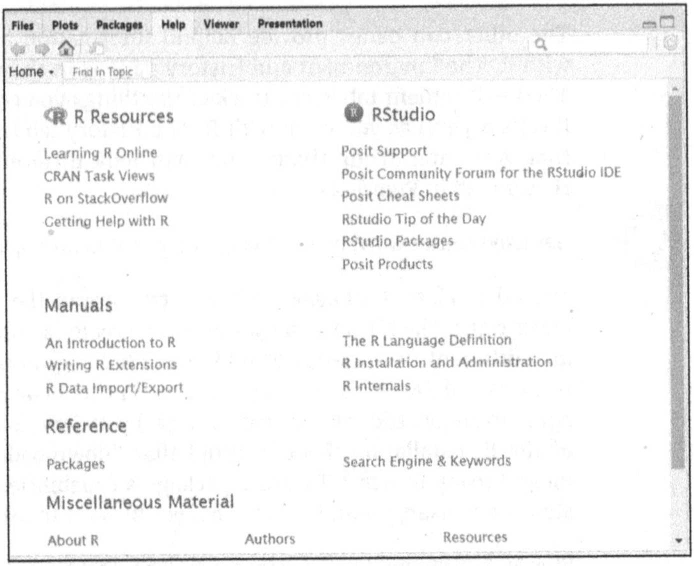

FIGURE 2-3: The RStudio Help tab.

To tap into the full power of RStudio as an IDE, click the icon in the upper-right corner of the Console pane. That changes the appearance of RStudio so that it looks like Figure 2-4.

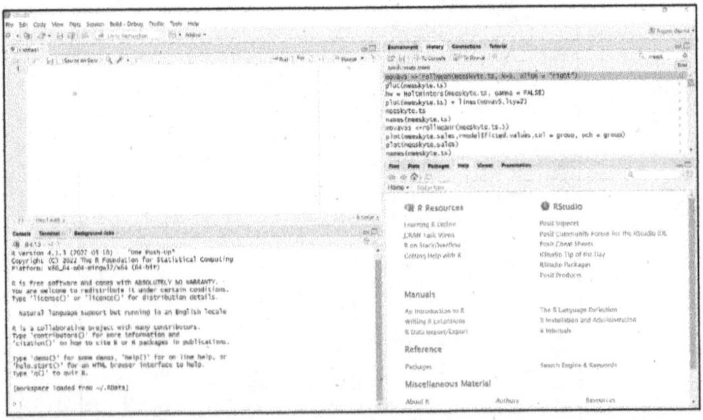

FIGURE 2-4: RStudio, after you click icon in the upper-right corner of the Console pane.

The top of the Console pane relocates to the lower left. The new pane in the upper left is the Scripts pane. You type and edit code in the Scripts pane and press Ctrl+Enter (Command+Return on the Mac), and then the code executes in the Console pane.

You can also choose Code ⇨ Run Selected Line(s).

TIP

A Session with R

Before you start working, choose File ⇨ Save As and then save as My First R Session. This relabels the tab in the Scripts pane with the name of the file and adds the .R extension. This also causes the filename (along with the .R extension) to appear on the Files tab.

The working directory

What exactly does R save, and where does R save it? What R saves is called the *workspace*, which is the environment you're working in. R saves the workspace in the *working directory*. In Windows, the default working directory is

```
C:\Users\<User Name>\Documents
```

If you ever forget the path to your working directory, type

```
> getwd()
```

in the Console pane, and R returns the path onscreen.

In the Console pane, you don't type the right-pointing arrowhead at the beginning of the line. That's a prompt.

TIP

My working directory looks like this:

```
> getwd()
[1] "C:/Users/Joseph Schmuller/Documents"
```

Note which way the slashes are slanted. They're opposite to what you typically see in Windows file paths. This is because R uses \ as an *escape character*, meaning that whatever follows the \ means something different from what it usually means. For example, \t in R means *Tab character*.

TIP

You can also write a Windows file path in R as

```
C:\\Users\\
```

If you like, you can change the working directory:

```
> setwd(<file path>)
```

Another way to change the working directory is to choose Session ➪ Set Working Directory ➪ Choose Directory.

So let's get started, already

And now for some R! In the Script window, type

```
x <- c(3,4,5)
```

and then Ctrl+Enter.

That puts the following line into the Console window:

```
> x <- c(3,4,5)
```

As I mention in an earlier Tip, the right-pointing arrowhead (the greater-than sign) is a prompt that R supplies in the Console pane. You don't see it in the Script pane.

What did R just do? The arrow sign says that x gets assigned whatever is to the right of the arrow sign. So the arrow-sign is R's *assignment operator*.

To the right of the arrow sign, the c stands for *concatenate*, a fancy way of saying "Take whatever items are in the parentheses and put them together." So the set of numbers 3, 4, 5 is now assigned to x.

REMEMBER

R refers to a set of numbers like this as a *vector*. (I tell you more on this in the later "R Structures" section.)

You can read that line of R code as "x gets the vector 3, 4, 5."

Type **x** into the Scripts pane and press Ctrl+Enter, and here's what you see in the Console pane:

```
> x
[1] 3 4 5
```

The 1 in square brackets is the label for the first value in the line of output. Here you have only one value, of course. What happens when R outputs many values over many lines? Each line gets a bracketed numeric label, and the number corresponds to the first value in the line. For example, if the output consists of 21 values and the 18th value is the first one on the second line, the second line begins with [18].

Creating the vector x causes the Environment tab to look like Figure 2-5.

FIGURE 2-5: The RStudio Environment tab, after creating the vector x.

Another way to see the objects in the environment is to type

```
> ls( )
```

Now you can work with x. First, add all numbers in the vector. Typing

```
sum(x)
```

in the Scripts pane (remember to follow with Ctrl+Enter) executes the following line in the Console pane:

```
> sum(x)
[1] 12
```

How about the average of the numbers in the vector x?

That's

```
mean(x)
```

in the Scripts pane, which (when followed by Ctrl+Enter) executes to

```
>  mean(x)
[1] 4
```

in the Console pane.

TIP

As you type in the Script pane or in the Console pane, you'll notice that helpful information pops up. As you gain experience with RStudio, you'll learn how to use that information.

As I show you in Chapter 6, *variance* is a measure of how much a set of numbers differs from their mean. What exactly is variance, and how do you calculate it? I'll leave that for Chapter 6. For now, here's how you use R to calculate variance:

```
>  var(x)
[1] 1
```

In each case, you type a command and R evaluates it and displays the result.

Figure 2-6 shows what RStudio looks like after all these commands.

To end a session, select File ⇨ Quit Session or press Ctrl+Q. As Figure 2-7 shows, a dialog box opens and asks what you want to save from the session. Saving the selections enables you to reopen the session where you left off the next time you open RStudio (although the Console pane doesn't save your work).

Pretty helpful, this RStudio.

REMEMBER

Moving forward, most of the time I don't say "Type this R code into the Script window and press Ctrl+Enter" whenever I take you through an example. I just show you the code and its output, as in the var() example.

REMEMBER

Also, sometimes I show code with the > prompt, and sometimes without. Generally, I show the prompt when I want you to see R code and its results. I don't show the prompt when I just want you to see R code that I create in the Script pane.

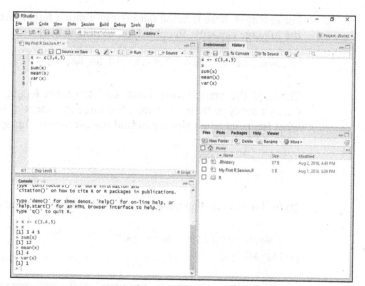

FIGURE 2-6: RStudio after creating and working with a vector.

Quit R Session

The following files have unsaved changes:

☑ Workspace image (.RData)
~/.RData

☑ My First R Session.R
~/My First R Session.R

Don't Save   Save Selected   Cancel

FIGURE 2-7: The Quit R Session dialog box.

Missing data

In the statistical analysis examples I provide, I typically deal with best-case scenarios in which the data sets are in good shape and have all the data they're supposed to have.

In the real world, however, things don't always go so smoothly. Oftentimes, you encounter data sets that have values missing for one reason or another. R denotes a missing value as NA (for Not Available).

For example, here is some data (from a much larger data set) on the luggage capacity, in cubic feet, of nine vehicles:

```
capacity <- c(14,13,14,13,16,NA,NA,20,NA)
```

Three of the vehicles are vans, and the term *luggage capacity* doesn't apply to them — hence, the three instances of NA. Here's what happens when you try to find the average of this group:

```
> mean(capacity)
[1] NA
```

To find the mean, you have to remove the NAs before you calculate:

```
> mean(capacity, na.rm=TRUE)
[1] 15
```

So the rm in na.rm means "remove" and =TRUE means "get it done."

Just in case you ever have to check a set of scores for missing data, the is.na() function does that for you:

```
> is.na(capacity)
[1] FALSE FALSE FALSE FALSE FALSE  TRUE  TRUE
    FALSE  TRUE
```

R Functions

In the preceding section, I use c(), sum(), mean(), and var(). These are examples of *functions* (blocks of code that accomplish specific tasks) built into R. Each one consists of a function name immediately followed by parentheses. Inside the parentheses are the *arguments*. In this context, "argument" doesn't mean "disagreement," "confrontation," or anything like that. It's just the math term for whatever a function operates on.

Even if a function takes no arguments, you still include the parentheses.

The four R functions I've shown you are pretty simple in terms of their arguments and their output. As you work with R, however, you encounter functions that take more than one argument.

R provides a couple of ways for you to deal with multiargument functions. One way is to list the arguments in the order in which they appear in the function's definition. R calls this *positional matching*.

Here's what I mean. The function substr() takes three arguments. The first is a string of characters like "abcdefg", which R refers to as a *character vector*. The second argument is a *start* position within the string (1 is the first position, 2 is the second position, and so on). The third is a *stop* position within the string (a number greater than or equal to the start position). In fact, if you type **substr** into the Script pane, you see a helpful pop-up message that looks like this:

```
substr(x, start, stop)

Extract or replace substrings in a character
    vector
```

where x stands for the character vector.

This function returns the substring, which consists of the characters between the start and stop positions.

Here's an example:

```
> substr("abcdefg",2,4)
[1] "bcd"
```

What happens if you interchange the 2 and the 4?

```
> substr("abcdefg",4,2)
[1] ""
```

This result is completely understandable: No substring can start at the fourth position and stop at the second position.

But if you *name* the arguments, it doesn't matter how you order them:

```
> substr("abcdefg",stop=4,start=2)
[1] "bcd"
```

Even this works:

```
> substr(stop=4, start=2,"abcdefg:")
[1] "bcd"
```

So when you use a function, you can place its arguments out of order, if you name them. R calls this *keyword matching*, which comes in handy when you use an R function that has many arguments. If you can't remember their order, just use their names and the function works.

TIP

If you ever need help for a particular function — substr(), for example — type **?substr** and watch helpful information appear on the Help tab.

User-Defined Functions

You can create your own functions in R. As you might imagine, that can get quite complicated. Here are the fundamentals. The form of an R function is

```
myfunction <- function(argument1, argument2,
    ... ){
statements
return(object)
}
```

Here's a simple function for computing the sum of the squares of three numbers:

```
sumofsquares <- function(x,y,z){
  sumsq <- sum(c(x^2,y^2,z^2))
  return(sumsq)
}
```

Type that snippet into the Scripts pane and highlight it. Then press Ctrl+Enter. The following snippet appears in the Console pane:

```
> sumofsquares <- function(x,y,z ){
+   sumsq <- sum(c(x^2,y^2,z^2))
+   return(sumsq)
+ }
```

Each plus-sign is a *continuation prompt*. It just indicates that a line continues from the preceding line.

And here's how to use the function:

```
> sumofsquares(3,4,5)
[1] 50
```

A *comment* is a way of annotating code. Begin a comment with the # symbol, which of course is an *octothorpe*. (What's that you say? "Hashtag"? Surely you jest.) This symbol tells R to ignore everything to the right of it.

Comments are very helpful for someone who has to read code that you've written. For example:

```
sumofsquares <- function(x,y,z){ # list the
  arguments
  sumsq <- sum(c(x^2,y^2,z^2))  # perform the
  operations
  return(sumsq)      # return the value
}
```

Just a heads-up: I don't add comments to lines of code in this book. Instead, I provide detailed descriptions. In a book like this, I feel that's the most effective way to get the message across.

R Structures

I mention in the "R Functions" section, earlier in this chapter, that an R function can have many arguments. It's also the case that an R function can have many outputs. To understand the possible outputs (and inputs, too), you must understand the structures that R works with.

Vectors

The *vector* is R's fundamental structure, and I showed it to you in earlier examples. It's an array of data elements of the same type. The data elements in a vector are called *components*. To create a vector, use the function c( ), as I did in the earlier example:

```
> x <- c(3,4,5)
```

Here, of course, the components are numbers.

In a character vector, the components are quoted text strings ("Moe", "Larry", and "Curly"):

```
> stooges <- c("Moe","Larry","Curly")
```

TECHNICAL STUFF

Strictly speaking, in the substr( ) example, "abcdefg" is a character vector with one element.

It's also possible to have a *logical* vector, whose elements are TRUE and FALSE, or the abbreviations T and F:

```
> z <- c(T,F,T,F,T,T)
```

To refer to a specific component of a vector, follow the vector name with a bracketed number:

```
> stooges[2]
[1] "Larry"
```

Numerical vectors

In addition to c( ), R provides seq( ) and rep( ) for shortcut numerical vector creation.

Suppose you want to create a vector of numbers from 10 to 30 but you don't feel like typing all those numbers. Here's how to do it:

```
> y <- seq(10,30)
> y
 [1] 10 11 12 13 14 15 16 17 18 19 20 21 22 23 24
    25 26
[18] 27 28 29 30
```

On my screen, and probably on yours too, all the elements in y appear on one line. The printed page, however, is not as wide as the Console pane. Accordingly, I separated the output into two lines. I do that throughout the book, where necessary.

R has a special syntax for a numerical vector whose elements increase by 1:

```
> y <- 10:30
> y
 [1] 10 11 12 13 14 15 16 17 18 19 20 21 22 23 24
    25 26
[18] 27 28 29 30
```

If you want the elements to increase in steps of 2, use seq like this:

```
> w <- seq(10,30,2)
> w
 [1] 10 12 14 16 18 20 22 24 26 28 30
```

You might want to create a vector of repeating values. If so, rep() is the function to use:

```
> trifecta <- c(6,8,2)
> repeated_trifecta <- rep(trifecta,4)
> repeated_trifecta
 [1] 6 8 2 6 8 2 6 8 2 6 8 2
```

Another way to use rep() is to supply a vector as the second argument. Remember from the earlier example that x is the vector (3,4,5) What happens if you supply x as the second argument for rep()?

```
> repeated_trifecta <- rep(trifecta,x)
> repeated_trifecta
[1] 6 6 6 8 8 8 8 2 2 2 2 2
```

The first element repeats three times; the second element, four times; and the third element, five times.

Matrices

A *matrix* is a two-dimensional array of data elements of the same type. In statistics, matrices are useful as tables that hold data. (Advanced statistics has other applications for matrices, but that's beyond the scope of this book.)

You can have a matrix of numbers:

5	30	55	80
10	35	60	85
15	40	65	90
20	45	70	95
25	50	75	100

or a matrix of character strings:

```
"Moe" "Larry" "Curly" "Shemp"

"Groucho" "Harpo" "Chico" "Zeppo"

"Ace" "King" "Queen" "Jack"
```

The numbers constitute a 5 (rows) x 4 (columns) matrix; the character strings matrix is 3 x 4.

To create the 5 x 4 numerical matrix, first you create the vector of numbers from 5 to 100 in steps of 5:

```
> num_matrix <- seq(5,100,5)
```

Then you use the dim() function to turn the vector into a two-dimensional matrix:

```
> dim(num_matrix) <-c(5,4)
> num_matrix
```

```
     [,1] [,2] [,3] [,4]
[1,]    5   30   55   80
[2,]   10   35   60   85
[3,]   15   40   65   90
[4,]   20   45   70   95
[5,]   25   50   75  100
```

Note how R displays the bracketed row numbers along the side, and the bracketed column numbers along the top.

Transposing a matrix interchanges the rows with the columns. In R, the t() function takes care of that:

```
> t(num_matrix)
     [,1] [,2] [,3] [,4] [,5]
[1,]    5   10   15   20   25
[2,]   30   35   40   45   50
[3,]   55   60   65   70   75
[4,]   80   85   90   95  100
```

The function matrix() provides another way to create matrices:

```
> num_matrix <- matrix(seq(5,100,5),nrow=5)
> num_matrix
     [,1] [,2] [,3] [,4]
[1,]    5   30   55   80
[2,]   10   35   60   85
[3,]   15   40   65   90
[4,]   20   45   70   95
[5,]   25   50   75  100
```

If you add the argument byrow=T, R fills the matrix by rows, like this:

```
> num_matrix <- matrix(seq(5,100,5),nrow=5,byrow=T)
> num_matrix
     [,1] [,2] [,3] [,4]
[1,]    5   10   15   20
[2,]   25   30   35   40
[3,]   45   50   55   60
[4,]   65   70   75   80
[5,]   85   90   95  100
```

How do you refer to a particular matrix component? You type the matrix name and then, in brackets, the row number, a comma, and the column number:

```
> num_matrix[5,4]
[1] 100
```

Factors

In Chapter 1, I describe four types of data: nominal, ordinal, interval, and ratio. In nominal data, numbers are just labels, and their magnitude has no significance.

Suppose you're doing a survey of people's eye color. As you record a person's eye color, you record a number: 1 = amber, 2 = blue, 3 = brown, 4 = gray, 5 = green, and 6 = hazel. One way to think of this process is that eye color is a *factor*, and each color is a *level* of that factor. So in this case, the factor eye-color has six levels.

Factor is R's term for a nominal variable (also known as *categorical variable*).

REMEMBER

Now imagine that you've used the numeric code to tabulate the eye colors of 14 people and then turned those codes into a vector:

```
> eye_color <- c(2,2,4,1,5,5,5,6,1,3,6,3,1,4)
```

Next, you use the factor() function to turn eye_color into a factor:

```
> feye_color <- factor(eye_color)
```

Finally, you assign the levels of the factor:

```
> levels(feye_color) <- c("amber","blue", "brown",
    "gray","green","hazel")
```

Now, if you examine the eye color data in terms of the factor levels, it looks like this:

```
> feye_color
[1] blue  blue   gray   amber green green green
    hazel amber
```

```
[10] brown hazel brown amber grayLevels: amber
    blue brown gray green hazel
```

Lists

In R, a *list* is a collection of objects that aren't necessarily of the same type. Suppose that in addition to the eye color of each person in the example in the preceding section, you collect an "empathy score" based on a personality test. The scale runs from 0 (least empathy) to 100 (most empathy). Here's the vector for these people's empathy data:

```
> empathy_score <- c(15,21,45,32,61,74,53,92,83,22,
  67,55,42,44)
```

You want to combine the eye color vector in coded form, the eye color vector in factor form, and the empathy score vector into one collection named eyes_and_empathy. You use the list() function for this task:

```
> eyes_and_empathy <- list(eyes_code=eye_color,
  eyes=feye_color, empathy=empathy_score)
```

Note that you name each argument (eyes_code, eyes, and empathy). This causes R to use those names as the names of the list components.

Here's what the list looks like:

```
> eyes_and_empathy
$eyes_code
 [1] 2 2 4 1 5 5 5 6 1 3 6 3 1 4

$eyes
 [1] blue  blue  gray  amber green green green
     hazel amber
[10] brown hazel brown amber gray
Levels: amber blue brown gray green hazel

$empathy
 [1] 15 21 45 32 61 74 53 92 83 22 67 55 42 44
```

As you can see, R uses the dollar sign ($) to indicate each component of the list. So, if you want to refer to a list component, you type the name of the list, the dollar sign, and the component-name:

```
> eyes_and_empathy$empathy
 [1] 15 21 45 32 61 74 53 92 83 22 67 55 42 44
```

How about zeroing in on a particular score, like the fourth one? I think you can see where this is headed:

```
> eyes_and_empathy$empathy[4]
[1] 32
```

Lists and statistics

Lists are important because numerous statistical functions return lists of objects. One statistical function is t.test(). In Chapter 10, I explain this test and the theory behind it. For now, just concentrate on its output.

I use this test to see if the mean of the empathy scores differs from an arbitrary number — 30, for example. Here's the test:

```
> t.result <- t.test(eyes_and_empathy$empathy,
    mu = 30)
```

Let's examine the output:

```
> t.result

    One Sample t-test

data:  eyes_and_empathy$empathy
t = 3.2549, df = 13, p-value = 0.006269
alternative hypothesis: true mean is not equal to 30
95 percent confidence interval:
 36.86936 63.98778
sample estimates:
mean of x
 50.42857
```

Without getting into the details, understand that this output, t.result, is a list. To show this, you use $ to focus on some of the components:

```
> t.result$data.name
[1] "eyes_and_empathy$empathy"
> t.result$p.value
[1] 0.006269396
> t.result$statistic
        t
3.254853
```

Data frames

A list is a good way to collect data. A data frame is even better. Why? When you think of data for a group of individuals — like the 14 people in the example in the earlier section — you typically think in terms of columns that represent the data variables (like eyes_code, eyes, and empathy) and rows that represent the individuals. And that's a data frame. If the terms *data set* or *data matrix* come to mind, you've pretty much got it.

The function data.frame() works with the existing vectors to get the job done:

```
> e <-
    data.frame(eye_color,feye_color,empathy_score)
> e
    eye_color feye_color empathy_score
1        2       blue          15
2        2       blue          21
3        4       gray          45
4        1      amber          32
5        5      green          61
6        5      green          74
7        5      green          53
8        6      hazel          92
9        1      amber          83
10       3      brown          22
11       6      hazel          67
12       3      brown          55
13       1      amber          42
14       4       gray          44
```

Want the empathy score for the seventh person? That's

```
> e[7,3]
[1] 53
```

How about all the information for the seventh person:

```
> e[7,]
  eye_color feye_color empathy_score
7         5      green            53
```

Extracting data from a data frame

Suppose you want to do a quick check on the average empathy scores for people with blue eyes versus people with green eyes versus people with hazel eyes.

The first task is to extract the empathy scores for each eye color and create vectors:

```
> e.blue <- e$empathy_score[e$feye_color=="blue"]
> e.green <- e$empathy_score[e$feye_color=="green"]
> e.hazel <- e$empathy_score[e$feye_color=="hazel"]
```

Note the double equal-sign (==) in brackets. This is a *logical operator*. Think of it as "if e$feye_color is equal to 'blue.'"

REMEMBER

The double equal-sign (a==b) distinguishes the logical operator ("if a equals b") from the assignment operator (a=b; "set a equal to b").

Next, you create a vector of the averages:

```
> e.averages <- c(mean(e.blue),mean(e.green),
  mean(e.hazel))
```

Then you use length( ) to create a vector of the number of scores in each eye-color group:

```
> e.amounts <- c(length(e.blue), length(e.green),
  length(e.hazel))
```

And then you create a vector of the colors:

```
> colors <- c("blue","green","hazel")
```

Now you create a three-column data frame with color in one column, the corresponding average empathy in the next column, and the number of scores in each eye color group in the last column:

```
> e.averages.frame <- data.frame(color=colors,
  average=e.averages, n=e.amounts)
```

As was the case with lists, naming the arguments assigns the argument names to the data frame components (the vectors, which appear onscreen as columns).

And here's what it all looks like:

```
> e.averages.frame
  color  average n
1  blue 18.00000 2
2 green 62.66667 3
3 hazel 79.50000 2
```

for Loops and if Statements

Like many programming languages, R provides a way of iterating through its structures to get things done. R's way is called the *for* loop. And, like many languages, R gives you a way to test against a criterion — the *if* statement.

The general format of a for loop is

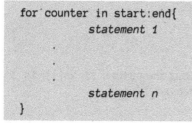

```
for counter in start:end{
        statement 1
        .
        .
        .
        statement n
}
```

As you might imagine, counter tracks the iterations.

The simplest general format of an if statement is

```
if(test){statement to execute if test is TRUE}
else{statement to execute if test is FALSE}
```

Here is an example that incorporates both. I have one vector xx:

```
> xx
[1] 2 3 4 5 6
```

And another vector yy with nothing in it at the moment:

```
> yy <-NULL
```

I want the components of yy to reflect the components of xx: If a number in xx is an odd number, I want the corresponding component of yy to be "ODD" and if the xx number is even, I want the yy component to be "EVEN".

How do I test a number to see whether it's odd or even? Mathematicians have developed *modular arithmetic,* which is concerned with the remainder of a division operation. If you divide *a* by *b* and the result has a remainder of *r*, mathematicians say that "a *modulo* b is r." So 10 divided by 3 leaves a remainder of 1, and 10 modulo 3 is 1. Typically, *modulo* gets shortened to *mod,* so that would be "10 mod 3 = 1."

Most computer languages write 10 mod 3 as mod(10,3). (Excel does that, in fact.). R does it differently: R uses the double percent sign (%%) as its *mod operator*:

```
> 10 %% 3
[1] 1
> 5 %% 2
[1] 1
> 4 %% 2
[1] 0
```

I think you're getting the picture: if xx[i] %% 2 == 0, then xx[i] is even. Otherwise, it's odd.

Here, then, is the `for` loop and the `if` statement:

```
for(i in 1:length(xx)){
    if(xx[i] %% 2 == 0){yy[i]<- "EVEN"}
    else{yy[i] <- "ODD"}
}

> yy
[1] "EVEN" "ODD"  "EVEN" "ODD"  "EVEN"
```

Chapter **3**

Digging Deeper Into R

t's time to delve more deeply into R. In this chapter, I tell you how to unlock R features that reside in packages. I also show you how to create R formulas that perform statistical analyses and how R imports and exports data.

Packages

A *package* is a collection of functions and data that augments R. If you're an aspiring data scientist and you're looking for data to work with, you'll find data frames galore in R packages. If you're looking for a specialized statistical function that's not in the basic R installation, you can probably find it in a package.

R stores packages in a directory called the *library*. How do you get a package into the library? Click the Packages tab in the Files, Plots, Packages, and Help pane. In the upcoming example, I use the well-known MASS package, which contains over 150 data frames from a variety of fields.

If you want to see what's in the MASS package, click on MASS in the Packages tab. (It's in the System Library section of this tab.) That opens a page on the Help tab, which appears in Figure 3-1.

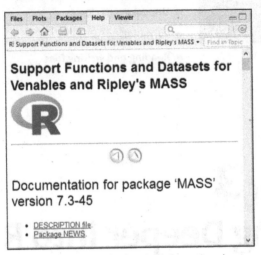

FIGURE 3-1: The Help tab, showing information about the MASS package.

Scrolling down shows the names of the data frames and functions. Clicking on the name of a data frame opens up a page of information about it.

Back on the Packages tab, you click the check box next to MASS to install the package. That causes this line to appear in the Console pane:

```
> library(MASS)
```

And the MASS package is installed.

One of the data frames in MASS is named anorexia. It contains weight data for 72 young female anorexia patients. Each patient completed one of three types of therapy. What does the data frame look like? You type this line into the Console pane:

```
> View(anorexia)
```

to open the view shown in Figure 3-2.

Looks like it's just waiting for you to analyze, doesn't it? I haven't discussed any statistical analysis yet, but you can work a bit on this data frame with what I've already shown you.

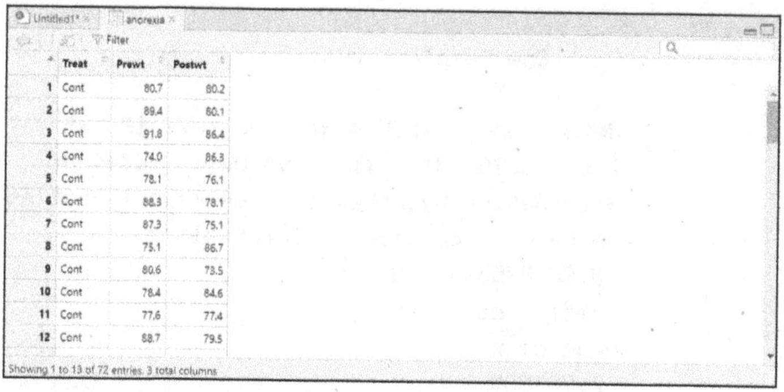

	Treat	Prewt	Postwt
1	Cont	80.7	80.2
2	Cont	89.4	80.1
3	Cont	91.8	86.4
4	Cont	74.0	86.3
5	Cont	78.1	76.1
6	Cont	88.3	78.1
7	Cont	87.3	75.1
8	Cont	75.1	86.7
9	Cont	80.6	73.5
10	Cont	78.4	84.6
11	Cont	77.6	77.4
12	Cont	88.7	79.5

FIGURE 3-2: The `anorexia` data frame in the MASS package.

The data frame provides the pre-therapy weight (`Prewt`) and post-therapy weight (`Postwt`) for each patient. What about the weight change? Can R calculate that for each patient? Of course!

```
> anorexia$Postwt-anorexia$Prewt
 [1]  -0.5  -9.3  -5.4  12.3  -2.0 -10.2 -12.2
  11.6  -7.1
[10]   6.2  -0.2  -9.2   8.3   3.3  11.3   0.0
  -1.0 -10.6
[19]  -4.6  -6.7   2.8   0.3   1.8   3.7  15.9
  -10.2   1.7
[28]   0.7  -0.1  -0.7  -3.5  14.9   3.5  17.1
  -7.6   1.6
[37]  11.7   6.1   1.1  -4.0  20.9  -9.1   2.1
  -1.4   1.4
[46]  -0.3  -3.7  -0.8   2.4  12.6   1.9   3.9
  0.1  15.4
[55]  -0.7  11.4  11.0   5.5   9.4  13.6  -2.9
  -0.1   7.4
[64]  21.5  -5.3  -3.8  13.4  13.1   9.0   3.9
  5.7  10.7
```

In Chapter 10, I describe a statistical test called the t-test, which is appropriate for this context. I use it here to see whether the pre-therapy/post-therapy weight change is different from 0. You would hope that, on average, the change is positive. Here's the t-test:

```
> t.test(anorexia$Postwt-anorexia$Prewt, mu=0)
```

```
    One Sample t-test

data:  anorexia$Postwt - anorexia$Prewt
t = 2.9376, df = 71, p-value = 0.004458
alternative hypothesis: true mean is not equal to 0
95 percent confidence interval:
 0.8878354 4.6399424
sample estimates:
mean of x
 2.763889
```

The t-test output shows that the average weight change was positive (2.763889 lbs). The high value of t (2.9376), along with the
low value of p (0.004458), indicates that this change is statistically significant. (What does *that* mean?) If I tell you any more, I'll
be getting ahead of myself. (See Chapter 10 for the details.)

Here's something else: I said that each patient completed one of
three types of therapy. Was one therapy more effective than the
others? Or were they about the same? Now I'd *really* be getting
ahead of myself! (That explanation is in Chapter 11, but see the
section "R Formulas," a little later in this chapter.)

More on Packages

The R community is extremely active. Its members create
and contribute useful new packages all the time to CRAN (the
Comprehensive R Archive Network). So it's not the case that every
R package is on the RStudio Packages tab.

When you find out about a new package that you think might
be helpful, it's easy to install it into your library. I illustrate by
installing DataEditR.

One way to install it is via the Packages tab. Click on the Install
icon in the upper left corner of the tab. This opens the Install
Packages dialog box, shown in Figure 3-3.

TIP

Another way to open the Install Packages dialog box is to select
Install Packages from the Tools menu in the menu bar at the top
of RStudio.

Install Packages

Install from: ? Configuring Repositories
Repository (CRAN)   ⌄

Packages (separate multiple with space or comma):

DataEditR

DataEditR brary:
C:/Users/jschm/Documents/R/win-library/4.1 [Default]   ⌄

☑ Install dependencies

                                    Install   Cancel

FIGURE 3-3: The Install Packages dialog box.

In the Packages field, I've typed DataEditR. Click Install, and the following line appears in the Console pane:

```
> install.packages("DataEditR")
```

It's difficult to see this line, however, because lots of other things happen immediately in the Console pane and in onscreen status bars. When all that has finished, DataEditR is on the Packages tab. The final step is to select the check box next to DataEditR in order to put it in the library. Then you can use the package. Figure 3-4 shows the Packages tab with DataEditR and the checked box.

Selecting the check box puts the following line in the Console pane:

```
> library(DataEditR)
```

Another way to start the installation process is to type

```
> install.packages("DataEditR")
```

TIP

directly into the Console pane.

After you install DataEditR and put it in your library, type

```
> data_edit(anorexia)
```

TIP

to open a window that enables you to interactively edit the data frame as you would edit a spreadsheet. When you finish editing, click Done.

Install | Update

Name	Description	Version	
curl	A Modern and Flexible Web Client for R	4.3.2	
data.table	Extension of 'data.frame'	1.14.2	
DataEditR	An Interactive Editor for Viewing, Entering, Filtering & Editing Data	0.1.5	
DBI	R Database Interface	1.1.3	
dbplyr	A 'dplyr' Back End for Databases	2.2.1	
dbscan	Density-Based Spatial Clustering of Applications with Noise (DBSCAN) and Related Algorithms	1.1-10	
deldir	Delaunay Triangulation and Dirichlet (Voronoi) Tessellation	1.0-6	
desc	Manipulate DESCRIPTION Files	1.4.2	
DescTools	Tools for Descriptive Statistics	0.99.46	
devtools	Tools to Make Developing R Packages Easier	2.4.4	
Diderot	Bibliographic Network Analysis	0.13	
didrooRFM	Compute Recency Frequency Monetary Scores for your Customer Data	1.0.0	
diffobj	Diffs for R Objects	0.3.5	
digest	Create Compact Hash Digests of R Objects	0.6.29	
doParallel	Foreach Parallel Adaptor for the 'parallel' Package	1.0.17	
downlit	Syntax Highlighting and Automatic Linking	0.4.2	
dplyr	A Grammar of Data Manipulation	1.0.10	
DT	A Wrapper of the JavaScript Library 'DataTables'	0.26	
dtplyr	Data Table Back-End for 'dplyr'	1.2.2	
e1071	Misc Functions of the Department of Statistics, Probability Theory	1.7-11	

FIGURE 3-4: The Packages tab after installing `DataEditR` and putting it in the library.

R Formulas

In Chapter 1, I discuss independent variables and dependent variables. I point out that, in an experiment, an independent variable is what a researcher manipulates and a dependent variable is what a researcher measures. In the earlier `anorexia` example, `Treat` (type of therapy) is the independent variable, and `Postwt-Prewt` (post-therapy weight minus pre-therapy weight) is the dependent variable. In practical terms, "manipulate" means that the researcher randomly assigned each anorexia patient to one of the three therapies.

In other kinds of studies, the researcher can't manipulate an independent variable. Instead, they note naturally occurring values of the independent variable and assesses their effects on a dependent variable. In the earlier eye color and empathy example, eye color is the independent variable and empathy score is the dependent variable.

The R *formula* incorporates these concepts and is the basis of many of R's statistical functions and graphing functions. This is the basic structure of an R formula:

```
function(dependent_var ~ independent_var,
    data=data_frame)
```

Read the tilde operator (~) as "is dependent on."

The anorexia data frame provides an example. To analyze the difference in the effectiveness of the three therapies for anorexia, I would use a technique called *analysis of variance*. (Here I go, getting ahead of myself!) The R function for this is named aov( ), and here's how to use it:

```
> aov(Postwt-Prewt ~ Treat, data=anorexia)
```

But this is just the beginning of the analysis. Chapter 11 has all the details, as well as the statistical thinking behind it.

Reading and Writing

Data can come from a variety of sources, so it's important to know how to import data from other formats, as well as how to export data to those formats.

The general form of an R function for reading a file is

```
> read.<format>("File Name", arg1, arg2, ...)
```

The general form of an R function for writing data to a file is

```
> write.<format>(dataframe, "File Name", arg1,
    arg2, ...)
```

In this section, I cover spreadsheets, CSV (comma-separated values) files, and text files. The <format> is either xlsx, csv, or table. The arguments after "File Name" are optional arguments that vary for the different formats.

Spreadsheets

The information in this section will be important to you if you've read my timeless classic, *Statistical Analysis with Excel For Dummies* (John Wiley & Sons). (Okay, so that was a shameless plug for my timeless classic.) If you have data on spreadsheets and you want to analyze with R, pay close attention.

The first order of business is to download the xlsx package and put it in the library. Check out the section "More on Packages," earlier in this chapter, for more on how to do this.

On my C: drive, I have a spreadsheet called Scores in a folder called Spreadsheets. It's on Sheet1 of the worksheet. It holds math quiz scores and science quiz scores for ten students.

To read that spreadsheet into R, the code is

```
> scores_frame <- read.xlsx("C:/Spreadsheets/
    Scores.xlsx", sheetName="Sheet1")
```

Here's that data frame:

```
> scores_frame
   Student Math_Score Science_Score
1        1         85            90
2        2         91            87
3        3         78            75
4        4         88            78
5        5         93            99
6        6         82            89
7        7         67            71
8        8         79            84
9        9         89            88
10      10         98            97
```

As is the case with any data frame, if you want the math score for the fourth student, it's just

```
> scores_frame$Math_Score[4]
[1] 88
```

The `xlsx` package enables writing to a spreadsheet, too. So, if you want your Excel-centric friends to look at the `anorexia` data frame, here's what you do:

```
> write.xlsx(anorexia,"C:/Spreadsheets/
  anorexia.xlsx")
```

This line puts the data frame into a spreadsheet in the indicated folder on drive C. In case you don't believe me, Figure 3-5 shows what the spreadsheet looks like.

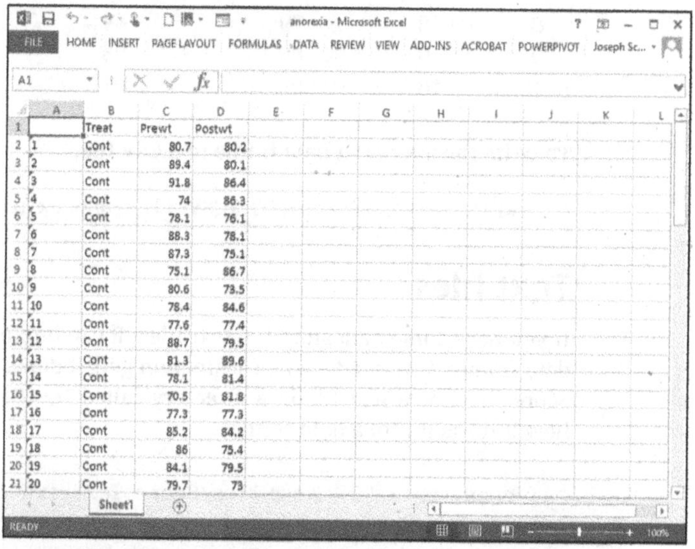

FIGURE 3-5: The `anorexia` data frame, exported to an Excel spreadsheet.

CSV files

The functions for reading and writing CSV files and text files are in the R installation, so no additional packages are necessary. A CSV file looks just like a spreadsheet when you open it in Excel. In fact, I created a CSV file for the Scores spreadsheet by saving the spreadsheet as a CSV file in the folder `CSVFiles` on drive C. (To see all the commas, you have to open it in a text editor, like Notepad++.)

Here's how to read that csv file into R:

```
> read.csv("C:/CSVFiles/Scores.csv")
   Student Math_Score Science_Score
1       1         85            90
2       2         91            87
3       3         78            75
4       4         88            78
5       5         93            99
6       6         82            89
7       7         67            71
8       8         79            84
9       9         89            88
10     10         98            97
```

To write the anorexia data frame to a CSV file,

```
> write.csv(anorexia,"C:/CSVFiles/anorexia.csv")
```

Text files

If you have some data stored in text files, R can import them into data frames. The read.table() function gets it done. I stored the Scores data as a text file in a directory called TextFiles. Here's how R turns it into a data frame:

```
> read.table("C:/TextFiles/ScoresText.txt",
  header=TRUE)
   Student Math_Score Science_Score
1       1         85            90
2       2         91            87
3       3         78            75
4       4         88            78
5       5         93            99
6       6         82            89
7       7         67            71
8       8         79            84
9       9         89            88
10     10         98            97
```

The second argument (header=TRUE) lets R know that the first row of the file contains column headers.

You use `write.table()` to write the `anorexia` data frame to a text file:

```
> write.table(anorexia, "C:/TextFiles/anorexia.
  txt", quote = FALSE, sep = "\t")
```

This puts the file `anorexia.txt` in the `TextFiles` folder on the `C:` drive. The second argument (`quote = FALSE`) ensures that no quotes appear, and the third argument (`sep = "\t"`) makes the file tab-delimited.

Figure 3-6 shows how the text file looks in Notepad. Full disclosure: In the first line of the text file, you have to press the Tab key once to position the headers correctly.

```
🗒 anorexia - Notepad                                                — ☐ ×
File  Edit  Format  View  Help
      Treat    Prewt    Postwt
1     Cont     80.7     80.2
2     Cont     89.4     80.1
3     Cont     91.8     86.4
4     Cont     74       86.3
5     Cont     78.1     76.1
6     Cont     88.3     78.1
7     Cont     87.3     75.1
8     Cont     75.1     86.7
9     Cont     80.6     73.5
10    Cont     78.4     84.6
11    Cont     77.6     77.4
12    Cont     88.7     79.5
13    Cont     81.3     89.6
14    Cont     78.1     81.4
15    Cont     70.5     81.8
16    Cont     77.3     77.3
17    Cont     85.2     84.2
18    Cont     86       75.4
19    Cont     84.1     79.5
20    Cont     79.7     73
21    Cont     85.5     88.3
22    Cont     84.4     84.7
23    Cont     79.6     81.4
24    Cont     77.5     81.2
25    Cont     72.3     88.2
26    Cont     89       78.8
27    CBT      80.5     82.2
28    CBT      84.9     85.6
29    CBT      81.5     81.4
30    CBT      82.6     81.9
```

FIGURE 3-6: The `anorexia` data frame as a tab-delimited text file.

In each of these examples, you use the full file path for each file. That's not necessary if the files are in the working directory. If, for example, you put the Scores spreadsheet in the working directory, here's all you have to do to read it into R:

```
> read.xlsx("Scores.xlsx","Sheet1")
```

Chapter **4**

Finding Your Center

I f you've ever worked with a set of numbers and had to figure out how to summarize them with a single number, you've faced a situation that statisticians deal with all the time. Where would this ideal "single number" come from?

A good idea might be to select a number from somewhere in the middle of the set. That number could then represent the entire set of numbers. When you're looking around in the middle of the set, you're looking at *central tendency*. You can address central tendency in a variety of ways.

Means: The Lure of Averages

We've all used averages. Statisticians refer to the average as the *mean*. The mean is an easy way to summarize your spending, your school grades, your performance in a sport over time.

I think you know how to calculate the mean, but I'll go through it anyway. Then I show you the statistical formula. My objective is that you understand statistical formulas in general, and then I'll show you how R calculates means.

A *mean* is just the sum of a set of numbers divided by how many numbers you added up. Suppose you measure the heights (in inches) of six 5-year-old children and find that their heights are

36, 42, 43, 37, 40, 45

The average height of these six children is

$$\frac{36+42+43+37+40+45}{6} = 40.5$$

The mean of this sample, then, is 40.5 inches.

A first attempt at a formula for the mean might be

$$\text{Mean} = \frac{\text{Sum of Numbers}}{\text{Amount of Numbers You Added Up}}$$

Formulas, though, usually involve abbreviations. A common abbreviation for "Number" is X. Statisticians usually abbreviate "Amount of Numbers You Added Up" as N. So the formula becomes

$$\text{Mean} = \frac{\text{Sum of } X}{N}$$

Statisticians also use an abbreviation for *Sum of* — the uppercase Greek letter for S. Pronounced "sigma," it looks like this: Σ. So the formula with the sigma is

$$\text{Mean} = \frac{\Sigma X}{N}$$

I'm not done yet. Statisticians abbreviate "mean," too. You might think that M would be the abbreviation, and some statisticians agree with you, but most prefer a symbol that's related to X. For this reason, the most popular abbreviation for the mean is $\bar{X}$, which is pronounced "X bar." And here's the formula:

$$\bar{X} = \frac{\Sigma X}{N}$$

I have to tie up one more loose end. In Chapter 1, I discuss samples and populations. Symbols in formulas have to reflect the distinction between the two. The convention is that English letters, like $\bar{X}$, stand for characteristics of samples, and Greek letters stand for characteristics of populations. For the population mean, the symbol is the Greek equivalent of *M*, which is μ. It's pronounced like "you" but with "m" in front of it. The formula for the population mean, then, is

$$\mu = \frac{\sum X}{N}$$

The Average in R: mean()

R provides an extremely straightforward way of calculating the mean of a set of numbers: mean(). I apply it to the example of the heights of six children.

First, I create a vector of the heights:

```
> heights <- c(36, 42, 43, 37, 40, 45)
```

Then I apply the function:

```
> mean(heights)
[1] 40.5
```

And there you have it.

What's your condition?

When you work with a data frame, sometimes you want to calculate the mean of just the cases (rows) that meet certain conditions, rather than the mean of all the cases. This is easy to do in R.

For the discussion that follows, I use the same Cars93 data frame that I use in Chapter 3. It's the one that has data for a sample of 93 cars from 1993. It's in the MASS package. So make sure you have the MASS package in your library. (Find MASS on the Packages tab and click its check box.)

Suppose I'm interested in the average horsepower of the cars made in the USA. First I select those cars and put their horsepowers into a vector:

```
Horsepower.USA <- Cars93$Horsepower[Cars93$Origin ==
    "USA"]
```

(If the right-hand part of that line looks strange to you, reread Chapter 2.)

The average horsepower is then

```
> mean(Horsepower.USA)
[1] 147.5208
```

Hmm, I wonder what that average is for cars not made in the USA:

```
Horsepower.NonUSA <- Cars93$Horsepower[Cars93$Origin
   == "non-USA"]
> mean(Horsepower.NonUSA)
[1] 139.8889
```

So the averages differ a bit. (Can we examine that difference more closely? Yes we can, which is just what I do in Chapter 11.)

Eliminate $ signs forthwith()

In the preceding R-code, the $ signs denote variables in the Cars93 data frame. R provides a way out of using the name of the data frame (and hence, the $ sign) each time you refer to one of its variables.

The function with() does this for you. The first argument is the data source, and the second argument is the function to apply to a variable in that data source.

To find the mean horsepower of USA cars in Cars93:

```
> with(Cars93, mean(Horsepower[Origin == "USA"]))
[1] 147.5208
```

This also skips the step of creating the Horsepower.USA vector.

How about multiple conditions, like the average horsepower of USA four-cylinder cars?

```
> with(Cars93, mean(Horsepower[Origin == "USA" &
   Cylinders ==4]))
[1] 104.0909
```

WARNING

R also provides the `attach()` function as a way of eliminating $ signs and keystrokes. Attach the data frame (`attach(Cars93)`, for example) and you don't have to refer to it again when you use its variables. Numerous R authorities recommend against this, however, as it can lead to errors.

Medians: Caught in the Middle

The mean is useful way to summarize a group of numbers. One drawback is that it's sensitive to extreme values.

Here, for example, are the reading speeds (in words per minute) for a group of children:

56, 78, 45, 49, 55, 62

The mean is

```
> reading.speeds <- c(56, 78, 45, 49, 55, 62)
> mean(reading.speeds)
[1] 57.5
```

Suppose the child who reads at 78 words per minute leaves the group and an exceptionally fast reader replaces him. Her reading speed is a phenomenal 180 words per minute:

```
> reading.speeds.new <- replace(reading.
  speeds,reading.speeds == 78,180)
> reading.speeds.new
[1]  56 180  45  49  55  62
```

Now the mean is

```
> mean(reading.speeds.new)
[1] 74.5
```

The new average is misleading. Except for the new child, no one else in the group reads nearly that fast. In a case like this, it's a good idea to use a different measure of central tendency — the median.

Median is a fancy name for a simple concept: It's the middle value in a group of numbers. Arrange the numbers in order, and the median is the value below which half the scores fall and above which half the scores fall:

```
> sort(reading.speeds)
[1] 45 49 55 56 62 78
> sort(reading.speeds.new)
[1]  45  49  55  56  62 180
```

In each case, the median is halfway between 55 and 56, or 55.5.

The Median in R: median()

So it's no big mystery how to use R to find the median:

```
> median(reading.speeds)
[1] 55.5
> median(reading.speeds.new)
[1] 55.5
```

With larger data sets, you might encounter replication of scores. In any case, the median is still the middle value. For example, here are the horsepowers for four-cylinder cars in Cars93:

```
> with(Cars93, Horsepower.Four <- Horsepower
  [Cylinders == 4])
> sort(Horsepower.Four)
 [1]   63   74   81   81   82   82   85   90   90   92   92
   92   92   92
[15]   93   96  100  100  100  102  103  105  110  110  110
   110 110 110
[29]  110 114 115 124 127 128 130 130 130 134 135
   138 140 140
[43]  140 141 150 155 160 164 208
```

You see quite a bit of duplication in these numbers — particularly around the middle. Count through the sorted values and you'll see that 24 scores are equal to or less than 110, and 24 scores are greater than or equal to 110, which makes the median

```
> median(Horsepower.Four)
[1] 110
```

Statistics à la Mode

One more measure of central tendency, the *mode*, is important. It's the score that occurs most frequently in a group of scores.

Nothing is complicated about finding the mode. Look at the scores and find the one that occurs most frequently, and you've found the mode. Do two scores tie for that honor? In that case, your set of scores has two modes. (The technical name is *bimodal*.)

Can you have more than two modes? Absolutely.

If every score occurs equally often, you have no mode.

The Mode in R

Base R does not provide a function for finding the mode. It does have a function called mode( ), but it's for something *much* different. Instead, you need a package called modeest in your library. (On the Packages tab, select Install, and then in the Install dialog box, type **modeest** in the Packages box and click Install. Then check its check box when it appears on the Packages tab.)

One function in the modeest package is called mfv( ) ("most frequent value"), and that's the one you need. Here's a vector with two modes (2 and 4):

```
> scores <- c(1,2,2,2,3,4,4,4,5,6)
> mfv(scores)
[1] 2 4
```

Chapter **5**

Deviating from the Average

Calculating the mean is a great way to summarize a set of numbers, but the mean might mislead you. How? By not giving you all the information you typically need. If you rely only on the mean, you might miss something important about the set of numbers.

To avoid missing important information, another type of statistic is necessary — a statistic that measures *variation*. Think of variation as a kind of average of how much each number in a group of numbers differs from the group mean. Several statistics are available for measuring variation. They all work the same way: The larger the value of the statistic, the more the numbers differ from their mean. The smaller the value, the less they differ.

Measuring Variation

Suppose you measure the heights of a group of children and you find that their heights (in inches) are

48, 48, 48, 48, and 48

Then you measure another group and find that their heights are

50, 47, 52, 46, and 45

If you calculate the mean of each group, you'll find they're the same — 48 inches. Just looking at the numbers tells you the two groups of heights are different: The heights in the first group are all the same, whereas the heights in the second vary quite a bit.

Averaging squared deviations: Variance and how to calculate it

One way to show the dissimilarity between the two groups is to examine the deviations in each one. Think of a "deviation" as the difference between a score and the mean of all the scores in a group.

Here's what I'm talking about. Table 5-1 shows the first group of heights and their deviations.

TABLE 5-1 **The First Group of Heights and Their Deviations**

Height	Height-Mean	Deviation
48	48-48	0
48	48-48	0
48	48-48	0
48	48-48	0
48	48-48	0

One way to proceed is to average the deviations. Clearly, the average of the numbers in the Deviation column is zero.

Table 5-2 shows the second group of heights and their deviations.

What about the average of the deviations in Table 5-2? That's . . . zero!

So now what?

TABLE 5-2 **The Second Group of Heights and Their Deviations**

Height	Height-Mean	Deviation
50	50-48	2
47	47-48	–1
52	52-48	4
46	46-48	–2
45	45-48	–3

Averaging the deviations doesn't help you see a difference between the two groups, because the average of deviations from the mean in any group of numbers is *always* zero. In fact, veteran statisticians will tell you that's a defining property of the mean.

The joker in the deck here is the negative numbers. How do statisticians deal with them?

The trick is to use something you might recall from algebra: A minus times a minus is a plus. Sound familiar?

So . . . does this mean that you multiply each deviation times itself and then average the results? Absolutely. Multiplying a deviation times itself is called *squaring a deviation*. The average of the squared deviations is so important that it has a special name: *variance*.

Table 5-3 shows the group of heights from Table 5-2, along with their deviations and squared deviations.

The variance — the average of the squared deviations for this group — is $(4 + 1 + 16 + 4 + 9)/5 = 34/5 = 6.8$. This, of course, is quite different from the first group, whose variance is zero.

To develop the variance formula for you and show you how it works, I use symbols to show all this. X represents the Height heading in the first column of the table, and $\bar{X}$ represents the mean.

TABLE 5-3 The Second Group of Heights and Their Squared Deviations

Height	Height-Mean	Deviation	Squared Deviation
50	50-48	2	4
47	47-48	−1	1
52	52-48	4	16
46	46-48	−2	4
45	45-48	−3	9

A deviation is the result of subtracting the mean from each number, so

$$(X - \bar{X})$$

symbolizes a deviation. How about multiplying a deviation by itself? That's

$$(X - \bar{X})^2$$

To calculate variance, you square each deviation, add them up, and find the average of the squared deviations. If N represents the number of squared deviations you have (in this example, five), the formula for calculating the variance is

$$\frac{\sum(X - \bar{X})^2}{N}$$

Σ is the uppercase Greek letter sigma, and it means "the sum of."

What's the symbol for variance? As I mention in Chapter 1, Greek letters represent population parameters, and English letters represent sample statistics. Imagine that our little group of five numbers is an entire population. Does the Greek alphabet have a letter that corresponds to V in the same way that μ (the symbol for the population mean) corresponds to M?

Nope. Instead, you use the *lowercase* sigma! It looks like this: σ. And on top of that, because you're talking about squared quantities, the symbol for population variance is σ^2.

Bottom line: The formula for calculating population variance is

$$\sigma^2 = \frac{\sum(X - \bar{X})^2}{N}$$

Sample variance

The variance formula I just showed you is appropriate if the group of five measurements is a population. Does this mean that variance for a sample is different? It does, and here's why.

If your set of numbers is a sample drawn from a large population, your objective is most likely to use the variance of the sample to estimate the variance of the population.

The formula in the preceding section doesn't work as an estimate of the population variance. Although the mean calculated in the usual way is an accurate estimate of the population mean, that's not the case for the variance, for reasons far beyond the scope of this book.

REMEMBER

It's pretty easy to calculate an accurate estimate of the population variance. All you have to do is use $N-1$ in the denominator rather than N. (Again, for reasons way beyond this book's scope.)

And because you're working with a characteristic of a sample (rather than of a population), you use the English equivalent of the Greek letter — s rather than σ. This means that the formula for the sample variance (as an estimate of the population variance) is

$$s^2 = \frac{\sum(X - \bar{X})^2}{N-1}$$

The value of s^2, given the squared deviations in the set of five numbers, is

(4 + 1 + 16 + 4 + 9)/4 = 34/4 = 8.5

So if these numbers

50, 47, 52, 46, and 45

are an entire population, their variance is 6.8. If they're a sample drawn from a larger population, the best estimate of that population's variance is 8.5.

Variance in R

Calculating variance in R is simplicity itself. You use the `var()` function.

```
> heights <- c(50, 47, 52, 46, 45)
> var(heights)
[1] 8.5
```

It calculates the estimated variance (with $N-1$ in the denominator). To calculate that first variance I showed you (with N in the denominator), I have to multiply this number by $(N-1)/N$. Using `length()` to calculate N, that's

```
> var(heights)*(length(heights)-1)/length(heights)
[1] 6.8
```

If I were going to work with this kind of variance frequently, I'd define a function `var.p()`:

```
var.p = function(x){var(x)*(length(x)-1)/
    length(x)}
```

And here's how to use it:

```
> var.p(heights)
[1] 6.8
```

REMEMBER

For reasons that will become clear later, I'd like you to think of the denominator of a variance estimate (like $N-1$) as *degrees of freedom*. Why? Stay tuned. (Chapter 11 reveals all!)

Back to the Roots: Standard Deviation

After you calculate the variance of a set of numbers, you have a value whose units are different from your original measurements. For example, if your original measurements are in inches, their variance is in *square* inches. This is because you square the deviations before you average them. So the variance in the five-score population in the preceding example is 6.8 square inches.

It might be hard to grasp what that means. Often, it's more intuitive if the variation statistic is in the same units as the original measurements. It's easy to turn variance into that kind of statistic. All you have to do is take the square root of the variance.

Like the variance, this square root is so important that it has a special name: standard deviation.

Population standard deviation

The *standard deviation* of a population is the square root of the population variance. The symbol for the population standard deviation is σ (sigma). Its formula is

$$\sigma = \sqrt{\sigma^2} = \sqrt{\frac{\sum(X - \bar{X})^2}{N}}$$

For this 5-score population of measurements (in inches):

   50, 47, 52, 46, and 45

the population variance is 6.8 square inches, and the population standard deviation is 2.61 inches (rounded off).

Sample standard deviation

The standard deviation of a sample — an estimate of the standard deviation of a population — is the square root of the sample variance. Its symbol is *s* and its formula is

$$s = \sqrt{s^2} = \sqrt{\frac{\sum(X - \bar{X})^2}{N-1}}$$

For this sample of measurements (in inches):

   50, 47, 52, 46, and 45

the estimated population variance is 8.4 square inches, and the estimated population standard deviation is 2.92 inches (rounded off).

Standard Deviation in R

As is the case with variance, using R to compute the standard deviation is easy: You use the sd( ) function. And like its variance counterpart, sd( ) calculates s, not σ:

```
> sd(heights)
[1] 2.915476
```

For σ — treating the five numbers as a self-contained population, in other words — you have to multiply the sd( ) result by the square root of $(N-1)/N$:

```
> sd(heights)*(sqrt((length(heights)-1)/
    length(heights)))
[1] 2.607681
```

Again, if you're going to use this one frequently, defining a function is a good idea:

```
sd.p=function(x){sd(x)*sqrt((length(x)-1)/
    length(x))}
```

And here's how you use this function:

```
> sd.p(heights)
[1] 2.607681
```

Conditions, Conditions, Conditions . . .

In Chapter 4, I point out that with larger data frames, you sometimes want to calculate statistics on cases (rows) that meet certain conditions, rather than on all the cases.

As in Chapters 3 and 4, I use the Cars93 data frame for the discussion that follows. That data frame has data for a sample of 93 cars from 1993. You'll find it in the MASS package, so be sure you have the MASS package in your library. (Find MASS on the Packages tab and select its check box.)

I calculate the variance of the horsepowers of cars that originated in the USA. Using the with( ) function I show you in Chapter 4, that's

```
> with(Cars93, var(Horsepower[Origin == "USA"]))
[1] 2965.319
```

How many of those cars are in this group?

```
> with(Cars93, length(Horsepower[Origin == "USA"]))
[1] 48
```

How about the non-USA cars?

```
> with(Cars93, var(Horsepower[Origin == "non-USA"]))
[1] 2537.283
> with(Cars93, length(Horsepower[Origin == "non-
  USA"]))
[1] 45
```

I'll leave it as an exercise for you to compute the standard deviations for the USA cars and for the non-USA cars.

Chapter **6**

Standards, Standings, and Summaries

When you compare numbers, context is important. To make valid comparisons across contexts, you often have to convert numbers into standard units. In this chapter, I show you how to use statistics to do just that. Standard units show you where a score stands in relation to other scores within a group. I also show you other ways to determine a score's standing within a group, and I finish by showing you how to summarize data.

Catching Some Zs

A number in isolation doesn't provide much information. To fully understand what a number means, you have to take into account the process that produced it. To compare one number to another, they have to be on the same scale.

When you're converting currency, it's easy to figure out a standard. When you convert temperatures from Fahrenheit to Celsius, or lengths from feet to meters, a formula guides you.

When it's not so clear-cut, you can use the mean and standard deviation to standardize scores that come from different processes. The idea is to take a set of scores and use its mean as a zero-point, and its standard deviation as a unit of measure. Then you make comparisons: You calculate the deviation of each score from the mean, and then you compare that deviation to the standard deviation. You're asking, "How big is a particular deviation relative to (something like) an average of all the deviations?"

To make a comparison, you divide the score's deviation by the standard deviation. This transforms the score into another kind of score. The transformed score is called a *standard score*, or a *z-score*.

The formula for this is

$$z = \frac{X - \bar{X}}{s}$$

if you're dealing with a sample, and

$$z = \frac{X - \mu}{\sigma}$$

if you're dealing with a population. In either case, x represents the score you're transforming into a z-score.

A z-score can be positive, negative, or zero. A negative z-score represents a score that's less than the mean, and a positive z-score represents a score that's greater than the mean. When the score is equal to the mean, its z-score is zero.

When you calculate the z-score for every score in the set, the mean of the z-scores is 0, and the standard deviation of the z-scores is 1.

Standard Scores in R

The R function for calculating standard scores is called scale(). Supply a vector of scores, and scale() returns a vector of z-scores along with, helpfully, the mean and the standard deviation.

To show scale( ) in action, I isolate a subset of the Cars93 data frame. (It's in the MASS package. On the Packages tab, check the box next to MASS if it's unchecked.)

Specifically, I create a vector of the horsepowers of eight-cylinder cars from the USA:

```
> with(Cars93, Horsepower[Origin == "USA" &
  Cylinders == 8])
> Horsepower.USA.Eight
[1] 200 295 170 300 190 210
```

And now for the z-scores:

```
> scale(Horsepower.USA.Eight)
            [,1]
[1,] -0.4925263
[2,]  1.2089283
[3,] -1.0298278
[4,]  1.2984785
[5,] -0.6716268
[6,] -0.3134259
attr(,"scaled:center")
[1] 227.5
attr(,"scaled:scale")
[1] 55.83458
```

That last value is s, not σ. If you have to base your z-scores on σ, divide each element in the vector by the square root of $(N-1)/N$:

```
> N <- length(Horsepower.USA.Eight)
> scale(Horsepower.USA.Eight)/sqrt((N-1)/N)
            [,1]
[1,] -0.5395356
[2,]  1.3243146
[3,] -1.1281198
[4,]  1.4224120
[5,] -0.7357303
[6,] -0.3433408
```

```
attr(,"scaled:center")
[1] 227.5
attr(,"scaled:scale")
[1] 55.83458
```

Notice that scale() still returns *s*.

Where Do You Stand?

Standard scores show you how a score stands in relation to other scores in the same group. To do this, they use the standard deviation as a unit of measure.

If you don't want to use the standard deviation, you can show a score's relative standing in a simpler way. You can determine the score's rank within the group: In ascending order, the lowest score has a rank of 1, the second lowest has a rank of 2, and so on. In descending order, the highest score is ranked 1, the second highest 2, and so on.

Ranking in R

Unsurprisingly, the rank() function ranks the scores in a vector. The default order is ascending:

```
> Horsepower.USA.Eight
[1] 200 295 170 300 190 210
> rank(Horsepower.USA.Eight)
[1] 3 5 1 6 2 4
```

For descending order, put a minus sign (–) in front of the vector name:

```
> rank(-Horsepower.USA.Eight)
[1] 4 2 6 1 5 3
```

Tied scores

R handles tied scores by including the optional ties.method argument in rank(). To show you how this works, I create a new vector that replaces the sixth value (210) in Horsepower.USA. Eight with 200:

```
> tied.Horsepower <- replace(Horsepower.USA.
  Eight,6,200)
> tied.Horsepower
[1] 200 295 170 300 190 200
```

One way of dealing with tied scores is to give each tied score the
average of the ranks they would have attained. So the two scores
of 200 would have been ranked 3 and 4, and their average 3.5 is
what this method assigns to both of them:

```
> rank(tied.Horsepower, ties.method = "average")
[1] 3.5 5.0 1.0 6.0 2.0 3.5
```

Another method assigns the minimum of the ranks:

```
> rank(tied.Horsepower, ties.method = "min")
[1] 3 5 1 6 2 3
```

And still another assigns the maximum of the ranks:

```
> rank(tied.Horsepower, ties.method = "max")
[1] 4 5 1 6 2 4
```

A couple of other methods are available. Type **?rank** into the console window for the details (which appear on the Help tab).

Nth smallest, Nth largest

You can turn the ranking process inside out by supplying a rank
(like second-lowest) and asking which score has that rank. This
procedure begins with the sort() function, which arranges the
scores in increasing order:

```
> sort(Horsepower.USA.Eight)
[1] 170 190 200 210 295 300
```

For the second-lowest score, supply the index value 2:

```
> sort(Horsepower.USA.Eight)[2]
[1] 190
```

How about from the other end? Start by assigning the length of the vector to *N*:

```
> N <- length(Horsepower.USA.Eight)
```

Then, to find the second-highest score, it's

```
> sort(Horsepower.USA.Eight)[N-1]
[1] 295
```

Percentiles

Closely related to rank is the *percentile*, which represents a score's standing in the group as the percent of scores below it. If you've taken standardized tests like the SAT, you've encountered percentiles. An SAT score in the 80th percentile is higher than 80 percent of the other SAT scores.

Sounds simple, doesn't it? Not so fast. "Percentile" can have a couple of definitions, and hence, a couple (or more) ways to calculate it. Some define percentile as "greater than" (as in the preceding paragraph), some define percentile as "greater than or equal to." "Greater than" equates to "exclusive." "Greater than or equal to" equates to "inclusive."

The function quantile() calculates percentiles. If left to its own devices, it calculates the 0th, 25th, 50th, 75th, and 100th percentiles. It calculates the percentiles in a manner that's consistent with "inclusive" and (if necessary) interpolates values for the percentiles.

I begin by sorting the Horsepower.USA.Eight vector so that you can see the scores in order and compare with the percentiles:

```
> sort(Horsepower.USA.Eight)
[1] 170 190 200 210 295 300
```

And now the percentiles:

```
> quantile(Horsepower.USA.Eight)
     0%     25%     50%     75%    100%
 170.00 192.50 205.00 273.75 300.00
```

Notice that the 25th, 50th, and 75th percentiles are values that aren't in the vector.

To calculate percentiles consistent with "exclusive," add the type argument and set it equal to 6:

```
> quantile(Horsepower.USA.Eight, type = 6)
    0%    25%    50%    75%   100%
170.00 185.00 205.00 296.25 300.00
```

The default type (the first type I showed you) is 7, by the way. Seven other types (ways of calculating percentiles) are available. To take a look at them, type ?quantile into the Console window (and then read the documentation on the Help tab).

Moving forward, I use the default type for percentiles.

The 25th, 50th, 75th, and 100th percentiles are often used to summarize a group of scores. Because they divide a group of scores into fourths, they're called *quartiles*.

You're not stuck with quartiles, however. You can get quantile() to return any percentile. Suppose you want to find the 54th, 68th, and 91st percentiles. Include a vector of those numbers (expressed as proportions) and you're in business:

```
> quantile(Horsepower.USA.Eight, c(.54, .68, .91))
    54%    68%    91%
207.00 244.00 297.75
```

Percent ranks

The quantile() function gives you the scores that correspond to given percentiles. You can also work in the reverse direction — find the percent ranks that correspond to given scores in a data set. For example, in Horsepower.USA.Eight, 170 is lowest in the list of six, so its rank is 1 and its percent rank is 1/6, or 16.67 percent.

Base R doesn't provide a function for this, but it's easy enough to create one:

```
percent.ranks <- function(x){round((rank(x)/
   length(x))*100, digits = 2)}
```

The round() function with digits = 2 rounds the results to two decimal places.

Applying this function:

```
> percent.ranks(Horsepower.USA.Eight)
[1]   50.00   83.33   16.67 100.00   33.33   66.67
```

Creating Summaries

In addition to the functions for calculating percentiles and ranks, R provides a couple of functions that quickly summarize data and do a lot of the work I discuss in this chapter.

One is called fivenum(). This function, unsurprisingly, yields five numbers.

```
> fivenum(Horsepower.USA.Eight)
[1] 170 190 205 295 300
```

From left to right, that's the minimum, lower hinge (25th percentile), median, upper hinge (75th percentile), and maximum. Remember the quantile() function and the nine available ways (types) to calculate quantiles? This function's results are what type = 2 yields in quantile().

Another function, summary(), is more widely used:

```
> summary(Horsepower.USA.Eight)
   Min. 1st Qu.  Median    Mean 3rd Qu.    Max.
  170.0   192.5   205.0   227.5   273.8   300.0
```

It provides the mean along with the quantiles (as the default type in quantile() calculates them).

The summary() function is versatile. You can use it to summarize a wide variety of objects, and the results can look very different from object to object. I use it quite a bit in upcoming chapters.

The measures of central tendency and variability that I discuss in earlier chapters aren't the only ways of summarizing a set of scores. These measures are a subset of descriptive statistics. Some descriptive statistics — like maximum, minimum, and range — are easy to understand. Some — like skewness and kurtosis — are not.

This chapter covers descriptive statistics and shows you how to calculate them in R.

How Many?

Perhaps the fundamental descriptive statistic is the number of scores in a set of data. In earlier chapters, I work with length( ), the R function that calculates this number. As in earlier chapters, I work with the Cars93 data frame, which is in the MASS package. (If it isn't selected, click the check box next to MASS on the Packages tab.)

Cars93 holds data on 27 variables for 93 cars available in 1993. What happens when you apply length( ) to the data frame?

```
> length(Cars93)
[1] 27
```

So length( ) returns the number of variables in the data frame. The function ncol( ) does the same thing:

```
> ncol(Cars93)
[1] 27
```

I already know the number of cases (rows) in the data frame, but if I had to find that number, nrow( ) would get it done:

```
> nrow(Cars93)
[1] 93
```

If you want to know how many cases in the data frame meet a particular condition — like how many cars originated in the USA — you have to take into account the way R treats conditions: R attaches the label "TRUE" to cases that meet a condition, and "FALSE" to cases that don't. Also, R assigns the value 1 to "TRUE" and 0 to "FALSE."

To count the number of USA-originated cars, then, you state the condition and then add up all the 1s:

```
> sum(Cars93$Origin == "USA")
[1] 48
```

To count the number of non-USA cars in the data frame, you can change the condition to "non-USA", of course, or you can use != — the "not equal to" operator:

```
> sum(Cars93$Origin != "USA")
[1] 45
```

More complex conditions are possible. For the number of four-cylinder USA cars:

```
> with(Cars93, sum(Origin == "USA" & Cylinders ==
  4))
[1] 22
```

To calculate the number of elements in a vector, length( ), as you may have read earlier, is the function to use. Here is a vector of horsepowers for four-cylinder USA cars:

```
> Horsepower.USA.Four <- with(Cars93,
  Horsepower[Origin == "USA" & Cylinders == 4])
```

and here's the number of horsepower values in that vector:

```
> length(Horsepower.USA.Four)
[1] 22
```

The High and the Low

Two descriptive statistics that need no introduction are the maximum and minimum value in a set of scores:

```
> max(Horsepower.USA.Four)
[1] 155
> min(Horsepower.USA.Four)
[1] 63
```

If you happen to need both values at the same time:

```
> range(Horsepower.USA.Four)
[1]   63 155
```

Summarizing a Data Frame

If you're looking for descriptive statistics for the variables in a data frame, the summary() function will find them for you. I illustrate with a subset of the Cars93 data frame:

```
> autos <- subset(Cars93, select = c(MPG.
  city,Type, Cylinders, Price, Horsepower))
> summary(autos)
    MPG.city              Type       Cylinders      Price
 Min.   :15.00    Compact:16    3    : 3    Min.   :
  7.40
 1st Qu.:18.00    Large  :11    4    :49    1st
  Qu.:12.20
 Median :21.00    Midsize:22    5    : 2    Median
  :17.70
 Mean   :22.37    Small  :21    6    :31    Mean
  :19.51
 3rd Qu.:25.00    Sporty :14    8    : 7    3rd
  Qu.:23.30
 Max.   :46.00    Van    : 9    rotary: 1    Max.
  :61.90
   Horsepower
 Min.   : 55.0
 1st Qu.:103.0
 Median :140.0
 Mean   :143.8
 3rd Qu.:170.0
 Max.   :300.0
```

The results will lay out on your screen a bit differently than they appear here.

Notice the maxima, minima, and quartiles for the numerical variables and the frequency tables for Type and for Cylinders.

Two functions from the Hmisc package also summarize data frames. To use these functions, you need Hmisc in your library. (On the Packages tab, click Install and type **Hmisc** into the Packages box in the Install dialog box. Then click Install.) After it's installed, be sure to select the Hmisc check box on the Packages tab.

One function, describe.data.frame(), provides output that's a bit more extensive than what you get from summary():

```
> describe (autos)
autos

 5  Variables      93  Observations
───────────────────────────────────────────────────────
MPG.city
        n missing  unique    Info    Mean    .05
    .10
       93       0      21    0.99   22.37   16.6
    17.0
     .25    .50     .75     .90     .95
    18.0   21.0    25.0    29.0    31.4

lowest : 15 16 17 18 19, highest: 32 33 39 42 46
───────────────────────────────────────────────────────
Type
        n missing  unique
       93       0       6

            Compact Large Midsize Small Sporty Van
Frequency        16    11      22    21     14   9
%                17    12      24    23     15  10
───────────────────────────────────────────────────────
Cylinders
        n missing  unique
       93       0       6


              3   4  5  6 8 rotary
Frequency 3  49  2 31 7      1
%         3  53  2 33 8      1
───────────────────────────────────────────────────────
```

```
Price
       n missing  unique    Info    Mean     .05
  .10
      93        0      81       1   19.51    8.52
 9.84
    .25      .50     .75     .90     .95
  12.20   17.70   23.30   33.62   36.74

lowest :  7.4  8.0  8.3  8.4  8.6
highest: 37.7 38.0 40.1 47.9 61.9
```

```
Horsepower
       n missing  unique    Info    Mean     .05
  .10
      93        0      57       1   143.8    78.2
 86.0
    .25      .50     .75     .90     .95
  103.0   140.0   170.0   206.8   237.0

lowest :  55  63  70  73  74, highest: 225 255 278
  295 300
```

A value labeled Info appears in the summaries of the numerical variables. That value is related to the number of tied scores — the greater the number of ties, the lower the value of Info. (The calculation of the value is fairly complicated.)

Chapter **7**
What's Normal?

O ne of the main jobs of a statistician is to estimate char-acteristics of a population. The job becomes easier if the statistician can make some assumptions about the popu-lations he or she studies.

Here's an assumption that works over and over again: A specific attribute, ability, or trait is distributed throughout a population so that (1) most people have an average or near-average amount of the attribute, and (2) progressively fewer people have increas-ingly extreme amounts of the attribute. In this chapter, I discuss this assumption and its implications for statistics. I also discuss R functions related to this assumption.

Hitting the Curve

It's possible to capture this assumption in a graphical way. Figure 7-1 shows the well-known *bell curve* that describes the distribution of a wide variety of attributes. The horizontal axis represents measurements of the ability under consideration. A vertical line drawn down the center of the curve would corre-spond to the average of the measurements.

Digging deeper

On the horizontal axis of Figure 7-1 you see x, and on the vertical axis, *f(x)*. What do these symbols mean? The horizontal axis, as I mention, represents measurements, so think of each measurement as an x.

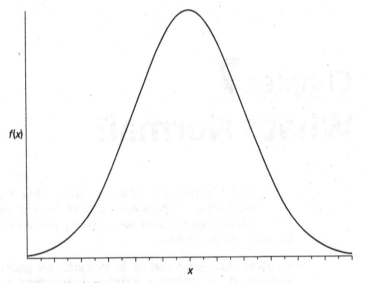

FIGURE 7-1: The bell curve.

The explanation of *f(x)* is a little more involved. A mathematical relationship between x and *f(x)* creates the bell curve and enables you to visualize it. The relationship is rather complex, and I won't burden you with it. Just understand that *f(x)* represents the height of the curve for a specified value of x. This means that you supply a value for x (and for a couple of other things), and then that complex relationship returns a value of *f(x)*.

Let me get into specifics. The formal name for "bell curve" is *normal distribution*. The term *f(x)* is called *probability density*, so a normal distribution is an example of a *probability density function*. Rather than give you a technical definition of probability density, I ask you to think of probability density as something that allows you to think about area under the curve as probability. Probability of . . . what? That's coming up in the next subsection.

Parameters of a normal distribution

You often hear people talk about "*the* normal distribution." That's a misnomer. It's really a *family* of distributions. The members of the family differ from one another in terms of two parameters — yes, *parameters* because I'm talking about populations. Those two parameters are the mean (μ) and the standard deviation (σ). The *mean* tells you where the center of the distribution is, and the *standard deviation* tells you how spread out the distribution is around the mean. The mean is in the middle of the distribution. Every member of the normal distribution family is symmetric — the left side of the distribution is a mirror image of the right.

The characteristics of the normal distribution family are well known to statisticians. More important, you can apply those characteristics to your work.

How? This brings me back to probability. You can find some useful probabilities if you

 » Can lay out a line that represents the scale of the attribute you're measuring (the x-axis, in other words)

 » Can indicate on the line where the mean of the measurements is

 » Know the standard deviation

 » Can assume that the attribute is normally distributed throughout the population

I'll work with IQ scores to show you what I mean. Scores on the IQ test follow a normal distribution. The mean of the distribution of these scores is 100, and the standard deviation of one version of the test is 15. Figure 7-2 shows the probability density for this distribution.

As Figure 7-2 shows, I've laid out a line for the IQ scale (the x-axis). Each point on the line represents an IQ score. With the mean (100) as the reference point, I've marked off every 15 points (the standard deviation). I've drawn a dashed line from the mean up to $f(100)$ (the height of the distribution where x = 100) and drawn a dashed line from each standard deviation point.

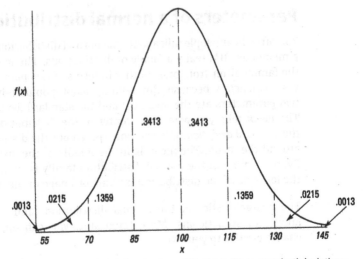

FIGURE 7-2: The normal distribution of IQ, divided into standard deviations.

The figure also shows the proportion of area bounded by the curve and the horizontal axis, and by successive pairs of standard deviations. It also shows the proportion beyond three standard deviations on either side (55 and 145). Note that the curve never touches the horizontal. It gets closer and closer, but it never touches. (Mathematicians say that the curve is *asymptotic* to the horizontal.)

So between the mean and one standard deviation — between 100 and 115 — are .3413 (or 34.13 percent) of the scores in the population. Another way to say this: The probability that an IQ score is between 100 and 115 is .3413. At the extremes, in the tails of the distribution, .0013 (.13 percent) of the scores are on each side (less than 55 or greater than 145).

The proportions in Figure 7-2 hold for every member of the normal distribution family, not just for IQ scores.

REMEMBER

Distributions in R

The normal distribution family is one of many distribution families baked into R. Dealing with these families is intuitive. Follow these guidelines:

- Begin with the distribution family's name in R (norm for the normal family, for example).

- To the beginning of the family name, add d to work with the probability density function. For the probability density function for the normal family, then, it's dnorm( ).

- For the cumulative density function (CDF), add p (pnorm( ), for example).

- For quantiles, add q (qnorm( ), which in mathematical terms is the *inverse* of the CDF).

- To generate random numbers from a distribution, add r. So rnorm( ) generates random numbers from a member of the normal distribution family.

Normal density function

When working with any normal distribution function, you have to let the function know which member of the normal distribution family you're interested in. You do that by specifying the mean and the standard deviation.

So, if you happen to need the height of the IQ distribution for IQ = 100, here's how to find it:

```
> dnorm(100,m=100,s=15)
[1] 0.02659615
```

REMEMBER

This does *not* mean that the probability of finding an IQ score of 100 is .027. Probability density is *not* the same as probability. With a probability density function, it only makes sense to talk about the probability of a score between two boundaries — like the probability of a score between 100 and 115.

Cumulative density function

The cumulative density function pnorm(x,m,s) returns the probability of a score less than x in a normal distribution with mean m and standard deviation s.

As you'd expect from Figure 7-2:

```
> pnorm(100,m=100,s=15)
[1] 0.5
```

How about the probability of less than 85?

```
> pnorm(85,m=100,s=15)
[1] 0.1586553
```

If you want to find the probability of a score greater than 85, pnorm() can handle that, too. It has an argument called lower. tail whose default value, TRUE, returns the probability of "less than." For "greater than," set the value to FALSE:

```
> pnorm(85,m=100,s=15, lower.tail = FALSE)
[1] 0.8413447
```

Quantiles of normal distributions

The qnorm() function is the inverse of pnorm(). Give qnorm() an area, and it returns the score that cuts off that area (to the left) in the specified normal distribution:

```
> qnorm(0.1586553,m=100,s=15)
[1] 85
```

The area (to the left), of course, is a percentile (described in Chapter 6).

To find a score that cuts off an indicated area to the right:

```
> qnorm(0.1586553,m=100,s=15, lower.tail = FALSE)
[1] 115
```

You're typically not concerned with the 15.86553rd percentile. Usually, it's quartiles that attract your attention:

```
> qnorm(c(0,.25,.50,.75,1.00),m=100,s=15)
[1]      -Inf  89.88265 100.00000 110.11735
   Inf
```

The 0th and 100th percentiles (–Infinity and Infinity) show that the CDF never completely touches the x-axis nor reaches an exact maximum. The middle quartiles are of greatest interest, and best if rounded:

```
> round(qnorm(c(.25,.50,.75),m=100,s=15))
[1]  90 100 110
```

Random sampling

The rnorm() function generates random numbers from a normal distribution.

Here are five random numbers from the IQ distribution:

```
> rnorm(5,m=100,s=15)
[1] 127.02944  75.18125  66.49264 113.98305
    103.39766
```

Here's what happens when you run that again:

```
> rnorm(5,m=100,s=15)
[1] 73.73596 91.79841 82.33299 81.59029 73.40033
```

Yes, the numbers are all different. (In fact, when you run rnorm(), I can almost guarantee your numbers will be different from mine.) Each time you run the function it generates a new set of random numbers. The randomization process starts with a number called a *seed*. If you want to reproduce randomization results, use the set.seed() function to set the seed to a particular number before randomizing:

```
> set.seed(7637060)
> rnorm(5,m=100,s=15)
[1]  71.99120  98.67231  92.68848 103.42207
    99.61904
```

If you set the seed to that same number the next time you randomize, you get the same results:

```
> set.seed(7637060)
> rnorm(5,m=100,s=15)
[1]  71.99120  98.67231  92.68848 103.42207
    99.61904
```

If you don't, you won't.

A Distinguished Member of the Family

To standardize a set of scores so that you can compare them to other sets of scores, you convert each one to a z-score. (I discuss z-scores in Chapter 6.) The formula for converting a score to a z-score (also known as a standard score) is

$$z = \frac{x - \mu}{\sigma}$$

The idea is to use the standard deviation as a unit of measure. Now, if you standardize all the scores in a normal distribution, you have a normal distribution of z-scores. Any set of z-scores (normally distributed or not) has a mean of 0 and a standard deviation of 1. If a normal distribution has those parameters, it's a *standard normal distribution* — a normal distribution of standard scores.

The standard normal distribution in R

Working with the standard normal distribution in R couldn't be easier. The only change you make to the four norm functions is to not specify a mean and a standard deviation — the defaults are 0 and 1.

Here are some examples:

```
> dnorm(0)
[1] 0.3989423
> pnorm(0)
[1] 0.5
> qnorm(c(.25,.50,.75))
[1] -0.6744898  0.0000000  0.6744898
> rnorm(5)
[1] -0.4280188 -0.9085506  0.6746574  1.0728058
    -1.2646055
```

Chapter **8**

The Confidence Game: Estimation

"**P**opulation" and "sample" are pretty easy concepts to understand. A *population* is a huge collection of individuals, and a *sample* is a group of individuals you draw from a population. Measure the sample-members on some trait or attribute, calculate statistics that summarize the sample, and you're off and running.

In addition to those summary statistics, you can use the statistics to estimate the population parameters. This is a big deal: Just on the basis of a small percentage of individuals from the population, you can draw a picture of the entire population.

How definitive is that picture? In other words, how much confidence can you have in your estimates? To answer this question, you have to have a context for your estimates. How probable are they? How likely is the true value of a parameter to be within a particular lower bound and upper bound?

In this chapter, I introduce the context for estimates, show how that context plays into confidence in those estimates, and show you how to use R to calculate confidence levels.

Understanding Sampling Distributions

So you have a population, and you pull a sample out of this population. You measure the sample-members on some attribute and calculate the sample mean. Return the sample-members to the population. Draw another sample, assess the new sample-members, and then calculate *their* mean. Repeat this process again and again, always with the same number of individuals as in the original sample. If you could do this an infinite amount of times (with the same sample size every time), you'd have an infinite amount of means. Those sample means form a distribution of their own. This distribution is called *the sampling distribution of the mean.*

For a sample mean, this is the "context" I mention at the beginning of this chapter.

In general, *a sampling distribution is the distribution of all possible values of a statistic for a given sample size.*

REMEMBER I've italicized the definition for a reason: It's extremely important. After many years of teaching statistics, I can tell you that this concept usually sets the boundary line between people who understand statistics and people who don't.

To help clarify the idea of a sampling distribution, take a look at Figure 8-1. It summarizes the steps in creating a sampling distribution of the mean.

A sampling distribution — like any other group of scores — has a mean and a standard deviation. The symbol for the mean of the sampling distribution of the mean (yes, I know that's a mouthful) is $\mu_{\bar{x}}$.

The standard deviation of a sampling distribution is a pretty hot item. It has a special name: *standard error.* For the sampling distribution of the mean, the standard deviation is called *the standard error of the mean.* Its symbol is $\sigma_{\bar{x}}$.

REMEMBER

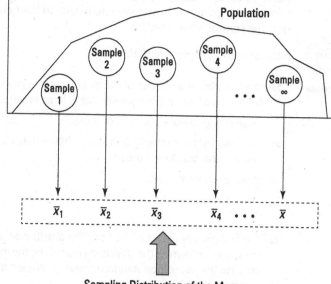

Sampling Distribution of the Mean

FIGURE 8-1: Creating the sampling distribution of the mean.

An EXTREMELY Important Idea: The Central Limit Theorem

The situation I asked you to imagine never happens in the real world. You never take an infinite amount of samples and calculate their means, and you never actually create a sampling distribution of the mean. Typically, you draw one sample and calculate its statistics.

So if you have only one sample, how can you ever know anything about a sampling distribution — a theoretical distribution that encompasses an infinite number of samples? Is this all just a wild-goose chase?

No, it's not. You can figure out a lot about a sampling distribution because of a great gift from mathematicians to the field of statistics: the central limit theorem.

REMEMBER

According to the *central limit theorem*:

>> The sampling distribution of the mean is approximately a normal distribution if the sample size is large enough.

Large enough means about 30 or more.

>> The mean of the sampling distribution of the mean is the same as the population mean.

In equation form, that's

$$\mu_{\bar{x}} = \mu$$

>> The standard deviation of the sampling distribution of the mean (also known as the standard error of the mean) is equal to the population standard deviation divided by the square root of the sample size.

The equation for the standard error of the mean is

$$\sigma_{\bar{x}} = \sigma / \sqrt{N}$$

Notice that the central limit theorem says nothing about the population. All it says is that if the sample size is large enough, the sampling distribution of the mean is a normal distribution, with the indicated parameters. The population that supplies the samples doesn't have to be a normal distribution for the central limit theorem to hold.

What if the population is a normal distribution? In that case, the sampling distribution of the mean is a normal distribution, regardless of the sample size.

Figure 8-2 shows a general picture of the sampling distribution of the mean, partitioned into standard error units.

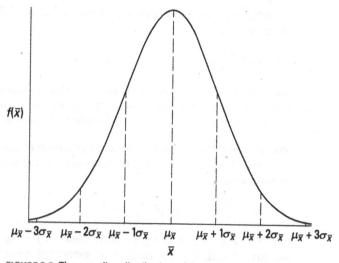

$\mu_{\bar{x}}-3\sigma_{\bar{x}}$ $\mu_{\bar{x}}-2\sigma_{\bar{x}}$ $\mu_{\bar{x}}-1\sigma_{\bar{x}}$ $\mu_{\bar{x}}$ $\mu_{\bar{x}}+1\sigma_{\bar{x}}$ $\mu_{\bar{x}}+2\sigma_{\bar{x}}$ $\mu_{\bar{x}}+3\sigma_{\bar{x}}$

$\bar{X}$

FIGURE 8-2: The sampling distribution of the mean, partitioned into standard error units.

Confidence: It Has its Limits!

I tell you about sampling distributions because they help answer the question I pose at the beginning of this chapter: How much confidence can you have in the estimates you create?

The procedure is to calculate a statistic and then use that statistic to establish upper and lower bounds for the population parameter with, say, 95 percent confidence. (The interpretation of confidence limits is a bit more involved than that, as you'll see.) You can do this only if you know the sampling distribution of the statistic and the standard error of the statistic. In the next section, I show how to do this for the mean.

Imagine a sample of 100 batteries. The mean battery life is 60 hours, with a standard deviation of 20 hours. What upper and lower bounds can we establish for this mean with 95 percent confidence?

The central limit theorem, remember, says that with a large enough sample (30 or more), the sampling distribution of the mean approximates a normal distribution. The standard error of the mean (the standard deviation of the sampling distribution of the mean) is

$$\sigma_{\bar{x}} = \sigma / \sqrt{N}$$

The sample size, N, is 100. What about σ? That's unknown, so you have to estimate it. If you know σ, that would mean you know μ, and establishing confidence limits would be unnecessary.

The best estimate of σ is the standard deviation of the sample. In this case, that's 20. This leads to an estimate of the standard error of the mean.

$$s_{\bar{x}} = s / \sqrt{N} = 20 / \sqrt{100} = 20/10 = 2$$

The best estimate of the population mean is the sample mean: 60. Armed with this information — estimated mean, estimated standard error of the mean, normal distribution — you can envision the sampling distribution of the mean, which is shown in Figure 8-3. Consistent with Figure 8-2, each standard deviation is a standard error of the mean.

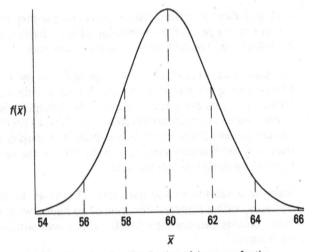

FIGURE 8-3: The sampling distribution of the mean for the battery example.

Now that you have the sampling distribution, you can establish the 95 percent confidence limits for the mean. Starting at the center of the distribution, how far out to the sides do you have to extend until you have 95 percent of the area under the curve? (For more on area under a normal distribution and what it means, see Chapter 7.)

One way to answer this question is to work with the standard normal distribution and find the z-score that cuts off 2.5 percent of the area in the upper tail. Then multiply that z-score by the standard error. Add the result to the sample mean to get the upper confidence limit; subtract the result from the mean to get the lower confidence limit.

Here's how to do all that in R. First, the setup:

```
> mean.battery <- 60
> sd.battery <- 20
> N <- 100
> error <- qnorm(.025,lower.tail=FALSE)*sd.
  battery/sqrt(N)
```

Then the limits:

```
> lower <- mean.battery - error
> upper <- mean.battery + error
> lower
[1] 56.08007
> upper
[1] 63.91993
```

Figure 8-4 shows these bounds on the sampling distribution.

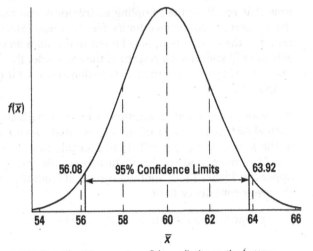

FIGURE 8-4: The 95 percent confidence limits on the battery sampling distribution.

Fit to a t

The central limit theorem specifies (approximately) a normal distribution for large samples. In the real world, however, you deal with smaller samples, and the normal distribution isn't appropriate. What do you do?

For small samples, the sampling distribution of the mean is a member of a family of distributions called the *t-distribution*. The parameter that distinguishes members of this family from one another is called *degrees of freedom*.

REMEMBER

As I said in Chapter 5, think of "degrees of freedom" as the denominator of your variance estimate. For example, if your sample consists of 25 individuals, the sample variance that estimates population variance is

$$s^2 = \frac{\sum(x-\bar{x})^2}{N-1} = \frac{\sum(x-\bar{x})^2}{25-1} = \frac{\sum(x-\bar{x})^2}{24}$$

The number in the denominator is 24, and that's the value of the degrees of freedom parameter. In general, degrees of freedom (df) = $N-1$ (N is the sample size) when you use the t-distribution the way I show you in this section.

Figure 8-5 shows two members of the t-distribution family (df = 3 and df = 10), along with the normal distribution for comparison. As the figure shows, the greater the df, the more closely t approximates a normal distribution.

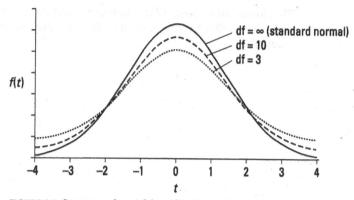

FIGURE 8-5: Some members of the t-distribution family.

To determine the lower and upper bounds for the 95 percent confidence level for a small sample, work with the member of the t-distribution family that has the appropriate df. Find the value that cuts off the upper 2.5 percent of the area in the upper tail of the distribution. Then multiply that value by the standard error.

Add the result to the mean to get the upper confidence limit; subtract the result from the mean to get the lower confidence limit.

R provides dt() (density function), pt() (cumulative density function), qt() (quantile), and rt() (random number generation) for working with the t-distribution. For the confidence intervals, I use qt().

In the batteries example:

```
> mean.battery <- 60
> sd.battery <- 20
> N <- 25
> error <- qt(.025,N-1,lower.tail=FALSE)*sd.
  battery/sqrt(N)
> lower <- mean.battery - error
> upper <- mean.battery + error
```

```
> lower
[1] 51.74441
> upper
[1] 68.25559
```

The lower and upper limits are 51.74 and 68.26. Notice that with the smaller sample, the range is wider than in the previous example.

Chapter 9

One-Sample Hypothesis Testing

Whatever your occupation, you often have to assess whether something new and different has happened. Sometimes you start with a population that you know a lot about (like its mean and standard deviation) and you draw a sample. Is that sample like the rest of the population, or does it represent something out of the ordinary?

To answer that question, you measure each individual in the sample and calculate the sample's statistics. Then you compare those statistics with the population's parameters. Are they the same? Are they different? Is the sample extraordinary in some way? Proper use of statistics helps you make the decision.

Sometimes, though, you don't know the parameters of the population that the sample came from. What happens then? In this chapter, I discuss statistical techniques and R functions for dealing with both cases.

Hypotheses, Tests, and Errors

A *hypothesis* is a guess about the way the world works. It's a tentative explanation of some process, whether that process occurs in nature or in a laboratory.

REMEMBER

Before studying and measuring the individuals in a sample, a researcher formulates hypotheses that predict what the data should look like.

Generally, one hypothesis predicts that the data won't show anything new or out of the ordinary. This is called the *null hypothesis* (abbreviated H_0). According to the null hypothesis, if the data deviates from the norm in any way, that deviation is due strictly to chance. Another hypothesis, the *alternative hypothesis* (abbreviated H_1), explains things differently. According to the alternative hypothesis, the data show something important.

After gathering the data, it's up to the researcher to make a decision. The way the logic works, the decision revolves around the null hypothesis. The researcher must decide to either reject the null hypothesis or to not reject the null hypothesis.

In *hypothesis testing*, you

>> Formulate null and alternative hypotheses
>> Gather data
>> Decide whether to reject or not reject the null hypothesis.

REMEMBER

Nothing in the logic involves *accepting* either hypothesis. Nor does the logic involve making any decisions about the alternative hypothesis. It's all about rejecting or not rejecting H_0.

Regardless of the reject-don't-reject decision, an error is possible. One type of error occurs when you believe that the data shows something important and you reject H_0, but in reality the data are due just to chance. This is called a *Type I error*. At the outset of a study, you set the criteria for rejecting H_0. In so doing, you set the probability of a Type I error. This probability is called *alpha* (α).

The other type of error occurs when you don't reject H_0 and the data is really due to something out of the ordinary. For one reason or another, you happened to miss it. This is called a *Type II error*. Its probability is called *beta* (β).

Note that you never know the true state of the world. (If you do, it's not necessary to do the study!) All you can ever do is measure the individuals in a sample, calculate the statistics, and make a decision about H_0. (I discuss hypotheses and hypothesis testing in Chapter 1.)

Hypothesis Tests and Sampling Distributions

In Chapter 8, I discuss sampling distributions. A sampling distribution, remember, is the set of all possible values of a statistic for a given sample size.

Also in Chapter 8, I discuss the central limit theorem. This theorem tells you that the sampling distribution of the mean approximates a normal distribution if the sample size is large (for practical purposes, at least 30). This works whether or not the population is normally distributed. If the population is a normal distribution, the sampling distribution is normal for any sample size. Here are two other points from the central limit theorem:

>> The mean of the sampling distribution of the mean is equal to the population mean.

The equation for this is

$$\mu_{\bar{x}} = \mu$$

>> The standard error of the mean (the standard deviation of the sampling distribution) is equal to the population standard deviation divided by the square root of the sample size.

This equation is

$$\sigma_{\bar{x}} = \sigma / \sqrt{N}$$

The sampling distribution of the mean figures prominently into the type of hypothesis testing I discuss in this chapter. Theoretically, when you test a null hypothesis versus an alternative hypothesis, each hypothesis corresponds to a separate sampling distribution.

Figure 9-1 shows what I mean. The figure shows two normal distributions. I placed them arbitrarily. Each normal distribution represents a sampling distribution of the mean. The one on the left represents the distribution of possible sample means if the null hypothesis is truly how the world works. The one on the right represents the distribution of possible sample means if the alternative hypothesis is truly how the world works.

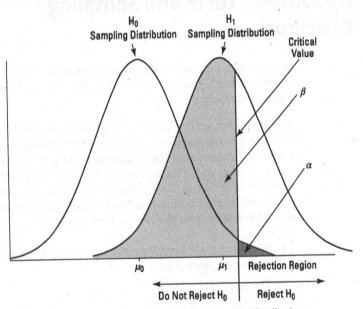

FIGURE 9-1: H_0 and H_1 each correspond to a sampling distribution.

These sampling distributions are appropriate when your work corresponds to the conditions of the central limit theorem: if you know that the population you're working with is a normal distribution or if you have a large sample.

Catching Some Z's Again

Here's an example of a hypothesis test that involves a sample from a normally distributed population. Because the population is normally distributed, any sample size results in a normally distributed sampling distribution. Because it's a normal distribution, you use z-scores in the hypothesis test:

$$z = \frac{\bar{x} - \mu}{\sigma / \sqrt{N}}$$

One more "because": Because you use the z-score in the hypothesis test, the z-score here is called the *test statistic*.

Suppose you think that people living in a particular zip code have higher-than-average IQs. You take a sample of nine people from that zip code, give them IQ tests, tabulate the results, and calculate the statistics. For the population of IQ scores, $\mu = 100$ and $\sigma = 15$.

The hypotheses are

$H_0: \mu_{ZIP\ code} \le 100$

$H_1: \mu_{ZIP\ code} > 100$

Assume that $\alpha = .05$. That's the shaded area in the tail of the H_0 distribution in Figure 9-1.

Why the $\le$ in H_0? You use that symbol because you'll reject H_0 only if the sample mean is larger than the hypothesized value. Anything else is evidence in favor of not rejecting H_0.

Suppose the sample mean is 108.67. Can you reject H_0?

The test involves turning 108.67 into a standard score in the sampling distribution of the mean:

$$z = \frac{\bar{x} - \mu}{\sigma / \sqrt{N}} = \frac{108.67 - 100}{\left(15 / \sqrt{9}\right)} = \frac{8.67}{\left(15 / 3\right)} = \frac{8.67}{5} = 1.73$$

Is the value of the test statistic large enough to enable you to reject H_0 with $\alpha = .05$? It is. The critical value — the value of z that cuts off 5 percent of the area in a standard normal distribution — is 1.645. The calculated value, 1.73, exceeds 1.645, so it's in the rejection region. The decision is to reject H_0.

This means that if H_0 is true, the probability of getting a test statistic value that's at least this large is less than .05. That's strong evidence in favor of rejecting H_0.

In statistical parlance, any time you reject H_0, the result is said to be *statistically significant*.

This type of hypothesis testing is called *one-tailed* because the rejection region is in one tail of the sampling distribution.

A hypothesis test can be one-tailed in the other direction. Suppose you have reason to believe that people in that zip code have lower-than-average IQs. In that case, the hypotheses are

$H_0: \mu_{ZIP\ code} \geq 100$

$H_1: \mu_{ZIP\ code} < 100$

For this hypothesis test, the critical value of the test statistic is -1.645 if $\alpha = .05$.

A hypothesis test can be *two-tailed*, meaning that the rejection region is in both tails of the H_0 sampling distribution. That happens when the hypotheses look like this:

$H_0: \mu_{ZIP\ code} = 100$

$H_1: \mu_{ZIP\ code} \neq 100$

In this case, the alternative hypothesis just specifies that the mean is different from the null-hypothesis value, without saying whether it's greater or whether it's less.

For a standard normal distribution, incidentally, the z-score that cuts off 2.5 percent in the right tail is 1.96. The z-score that cuts off 2.5 percent in the left tail is -1.96. The z-score in the preceding example, 1.73, does not exceed 1.96. The decision, in the two-tailed case, is to *not* reject H_0.

This brings up an important point. A one-tailed hypothesis test can reject H_0, while a two-tailed test on the same data might not. A two-tailed test indicates that you're looking for a difference between the sample mean and the null-hypothesis mean, but you don't know in which direction. A one-tailed test shows that you have a pretty good idea of how the difference should come out. For practical purposes, this means you should try to have enough knowledge to be able to specify a one-tailed test: That gives you a better chance of rejecting H_0 when you should.

Z Testing in R

An R function called z.test() would be great for doing the kind of testing I discuss in the previous section. One problem: That function does not exist in base R. Although you can find one in other packages, it's easy enough to create one and learn a bit about R programming in the process.

The function will work like this:

```
> IQ.data <- c(100,101,104,109,125,116,105,108,110)
> z.test(IQ.data,100,15)
z = 1.733
one-tailed probability = 0.042
two-tailed probability = 0.084
```

Begin by creating the function name and its arguments:

```
z.test' = function(x,mu,popvar){
```

The first argument is the vector of data, the second is the population mean, and the third is the population variance. The left curly bracket signifies that the remainder of the code is what happens inside the function.

Next, create a vector that will hold the one-tailed probability of the z-score you'll calculate:

```
one.tail.p <- NULL
```

Then you calculate the z-score and round it to three decimal places:

```
z.score <- round((mean(x)-mu)/(popvar/sqrt
    (length(x))),3)
```

Without the rounding, R might calculate many decimal places, and the output would look messy.

Finally, you calculate the one-tailed probability (the proportion of area beyond the calculated z-score), and again round to three decimal places:

```
one.tail.p <- round(pnorm(abs(z.score),lower.tail =
    FALSE),3)
```

Why put abs() (absolute value) in the argument to pnorm? Remember that an alternative hypothesis can specify a value below the mean, and the data might result in a negative z-score.

The next order of business is to set up the output display. For this, you use the cat() function. The name *cat* is short for *concatenate and print*, which is exactly what I want you to do here: Concatenate (put together) strings (like one-tailed probability =) with expressions (like one.tail.p), and then show that whole thing onscreen. I also want you to start a new line for each concatenation, and \n is R's way of making that happen.

Here's the cat statement:

```
cat(" z =",z.score,"\n",
        "one-tailed probability =", one.tail.p,"\n",
        "two-tailed probability =", 2*one.tail.p )}
```

The space between the left quote and z lines up the first line with the next two onscreen. The right curly bracket closes off the function.

Here it is, all together:

```
z.test = function(x,mu,popvar){
    one.tail.p <- NULL
    z.score <- round((mean(x)-mu)/(popvar/
    sqrt(length(x))),3)
    one.tail.p <- round(pnorm(abs(z.score),lower.
    tail = FALSE),3)
    cat(" z =",z.score,"\n",
        "one-tailed probability =", one.tail.p,"\n",
        "two-tailed probability =", 2*one.tail.p )}
```

Running this function produces what you see at the beginning of this section.

t for One

In the preceding example, you work with IQ scores. The population of IQ scores is a normal distribution with a well-known mean and standard deviation.

In the real world, however, you usually don't have the luxury of working with well-defined populations. You often don't know the population parameters, nor do you know if the population is normally distributed.

When that's the case, you use the sample data to estimate the population standard deviation, and you treat the sampling distribution of the mean as a member of a family of distributions called the t-distribution. You use t as a test statistic. In Chapter 8, I introduce this distribution and mention that you distinguish members of this family by a parameter called *degrees of freedom* (df).

The formula for the test statistic is

$$t = \frac{\bar{x} - \mu}{s/\sqrt{N}}$$

Think of df as the denominator of the estimate of the population variance. For the hypothesis tests in this section, that's $N-1$, where N is the number of scores in the sample. The higher the df, the more closely the t-distribution resembles the normal distribution.

Here's an example. FarKlempt Robotics, Inc., markets microrobots. The company claims that its product averages four defects per unit. A consumer group believes this average is higher. The consumer group takes a sample of nine FarKlempt microrobots and finds an average of seven defects, with a standard deviation of 3.12. The hypothesis test is

$H_0: \mu \leq 4$

$H_1: \mu > 4$

$\alpha = .05$

The formula is

$$t = \frac{\bar{x} - \mu}{s/\sqrt{N}} = \frac{7 - 4}{\left(3.12/\sqrt{9}\right)} = \frac{3}{\left(3.12/3\right)} = 2.88$$

Can you reject H_0? The R function in the next section tells you.

t Testing in R

I preview the t.test() function in Chapter 2 and talk about it in a bit more detail in Chapter 8. Here, you use it to test hypotheses.

Start with the data for FarKlempt Robotics:

```
> FarKlempt.data <- c(3,6,9,9,4,10,6,4,12)
```

Then apply t.test(). For the example, it looks like this:

```
t.test(FarKlempt.data,mu=4, alternative="greater")
```

The second argument specifies that you're testing against a hypothesized mean of 4, and the third argument indicates that the alternative hypothesis is that the true mean is greater than 4.

Here it is in action:

```
> t.test(FarKlempt.data,mu=4, alternative=
  "greater")

    One Sample t-test

data:  FarKlempt.data

t = 2.8823, df = 8, p-value = 0.01022
alternative hypothesis: true mean is greater than 4
95 percent confidence interval:
 5.064521      Inf
sample estimates:
mean of x
        7
```

The output provides the t-value and the low p-value shows that you can reject the null hypothesis with $\alpha = .05$.

This t.test() function is versatile. I work with it again in Chapter 10 when I test hypotheses about two samples.

Working with t-Distributions

Just as you can use d, p, q, and r prefixes for the normal distribution family, you can use dt() (density function), pt() (cumulative density function), qt() (quantiles), and rt() (random number generation) for the t-distribution family.

Here are dt() and rt() at work for a t-distribution with 12 df:

```
> t.values <- seq(-4,4,1)
> round(dt(t.values,12),2)
[1] 0.00 0.01 0.06 0.23 0.39 0.23 0.06 0.01 0.00
> round(pt(t.values,12),2)
[1] 0.00 0.01 0.03 0.17 0.50 0.83 0.97 0.99 1.00
```

For quantile information about the t-distribution with 12 df:

```
> quartiles <- c(0,.25,.50,.75,1)
> qt(quartiles,12)
[1]        -Inf -0.6954829  0.0000000  0.6954829
   Inf
```

The -Inf and Inf tell you that the curve never touches the x-axis at either tail.

To generate eight (rounded) random numbers from the t-distribution with 12 df:

```
> round(rt(8,12),2)
[1]  0.73  0.13 -1.32  1.33 -1.27  0.91 -0.48
   -0.83
```

All these functions give you the option of working with t-distributions not centered around zero. You do this by entering a value for ncp (the *noncentrality* parameter). In most applications of the t-distribution, noncentrality doesn't come up.

Chapter **10**

Two-Sample Hypothesis Testing

I n a variety of fields, the need often arises to compare one sample with another. Sometimes the samples are independent, and sometimes they're matched in some way. Each sample comes from a separate population. The objective is to decide whether these populations are different from one another.

Usually, this involves tests of hypotheses about population means. You can also test hypotheses about population variances. In this chapter, I show you how to carry out these tests, and how to use R to get the job done.

Hypotheses Built for Two

As in the one–sample case (see Chapter 9), hypothesis testing with two samples starts with a null hypothesis (H_0) and an alternative hypothesis (H_1). The null hypothesis specifies that any differences you see between the two samples are due strictly to chance. The alternative hypothesis says, in effect, that any differences you see are real and not due to chance.

It's possible to have a *one-tailed test*, in which the alternative hypothesis specifies the direction of the difference between the two means, or a *two-tailed test* in which the alternative hypothesis does not specify the direction of the difference.

For a one-tailed test, the hypotheses look like this:

$H_0: \mu_1 - \mu_2 = 0$

$H_1: \mu_1 - \mu_2 > 0$

or like this:

$H_0: \mu_1 - \mu_2 = 0$

$H_1: \mu_1 - \mu_2 < 0$

For a two-tailed test, the hypotheses are:

$H_0: \mu_1 - \mu_2 = 0$

$H_1: \mu_1 - \mu_2 \neq 0$

The zero in these hypotheses is the typical case. It's possible, how-ever, to test for any value — just substitute that value for zero.

To carry out the test, you first set α, the probability of a Type I error that you're willing to live with. (See Chapter 9.) Then you calculate the mean and standard deviation of each sample, sub-tract one mean from the other, and use a formula to convert the result into a test statistic. Compare the test statistic to a sam-pling distribution of test statistics. If it's in the rejection region that α specifies (again, see Chapter 9), reject H_0. If it's not, don't reject H_0.

Sampling Distributions Revisited

In Chapter 8, I introduce the idea of a sampling distribution — a distribution of all possible values of a statistic for a particular sample size. In that chapter, I describe the sampling distribution of the mean. In Chapter 9, I show its connection with one-sample hypothesis testing.

For two-sample hypothesis testing, another sampling distribution is necessary. This one is the sampling distribution of the difference between means.

The *sampling distribution of the difference between means* is the distribution of all possible values of differences between pairs of sample means with the sample sizes held constant from pair to pair. (Yes, that's a mouthful.) *Held constant from pair to pair* means that the first sample in the pair always has the same size, and the second sample in the pair always has the same size. The two sample sizes are not necessarily equal.

Within each pair, each sample comes from a different population. All samples are independent of one another so that picking individuals for one sample has no effect on picking individuals for another.

Figure 10-1 shows the steps in creating this sampling distribution. This is something you never do in practice. It's all theoretical. As the figure shows, the idea is to take a sample out of one population and a sample out of another, calculate their means, and subtract one mean from the other. Return the samples to the populations, and repeat over and over and over. The result of the process is a set of differences between means. This set of differences is the sampling distribution.

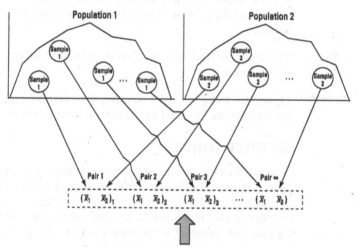

Sampling Distribution of the Difference Between Means

FIGURE 10-1: Creating the sampling distribution of the difference between means.

Applying the central limit theorem

Like any other set of numbers, this sampling distribution has a mean and a standard deviation. As is the case with the sampling distribution of the mean (see Chapters 8 and 9), the central limit theorem applies here.

According to the central limit theorem, if the samples are large, the sampling distribution of the difference between means is approximately a normal distribution. If the populations are normally distributed, the sampling distribution is a normal distribution even if the samples are small.

The central limit theorem also has something to say about the mean and standard deviation of this sampling distribution. Suppose that the parameters for the first population are μ_1 and σ_1, and the parameters for the second population are μ_2 and σ_2. The mean of the sampling distribution is

$$\mu_{\bar{x}_1 - \bar{x}_2} = \mu_1 - \mu_2$$

The standard deviation of the sampling distribution is

$$\sigma_{\bar{x}_1 - \bar{x}_2} = \sqrt{\frac{\sigma_1^2}{N_1} + \frac{\sigma_2^2}{N_2}}$$

N_1 is the number of individuals in the sample from the first population, and N_2 is the number of individuals in the sample from the second.

This standard deviation is called *the standard error of the difference between means.*

REMEMBER

Figure 10-2 shows the sampling distribution along with its parameters, as specified by the central limit theorem.

Zs once more

Because the central limit theorem says that the sampling distribution is approximately normal for large samples (or for small samples from normally distributed populations), you use the z-score as your test statistic. Another way to say "use the z-score as your test statistic" is "perform a z-test." Here's the formula:

$$z = \frac{(\bar{x}_1 - \bar{x}_2) - (\mu_1 - \mu_2)}{\sigma_{\bar{x}_1 - \bar{x}_2}}$$

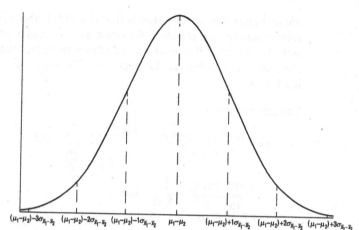

$(\mu_1-\mu_2)-3\sigma_{\bar{x}_1-\bar{x}_2}$ $(\mu_1-\mu_2)-2\sigma_{\bar{x}_1-\bar{x}_2}$ $(\mu_1-\mu_2)-1\sigma_{\bar{x}_1-\bar{x}_2}$ $\mu_1-\mu_2$ $(\mu_1-\mu_2)+1\sigma_{\bar{x}_1-\bar{x}_2}$ $(\mu_1-\mu_2)+2\sigma_{\bar{x}_1-\bar{x}_2}$ $(\mu_1-\mu_2)+3\sigma_{\bar{x}_1-\bar{x}_2}$

FIGURE 10-2: The sampling distribution of the difference between means, according to the central limit theorem.

The term $(\mu_1-\mu_2)$ represents the difference between the means in H_0.

This formula converts the difference between sample means into a standard score. Compare the standard score against a standard normal distribution — a normal distribution with $\mu = 0$ and $\sigma = 1$. If the score is in the rejection region defined by α, reject H_0. If it's not, don't reject H_0.

You use this formula when you know the value of σ_1^2 and σ_2^2.

Here's an example. Imagine a new training technique designed to increase IQ. Take a sample of nine people and train them under the new technique. Take another sample of nine people and give them no special training. Suppose that the sample mean for the new technique sample is 110.222, and for the no-training sample it's 101. The hypothesis test is

$H_0: \mu_1 - \mu_2 \leq 0$

$H_1: \mu_1 - \mu_2 > 0$

I'll set α at .05.

The IQ is known to have a standard deviation of 15, and I assume that standard deviation would be the same in the population of people trained on the new technique. Of course, that population doesn't exist. The assumption is that if it did, it should have the same value for the standard deviation as the regular population of IQ scores. Does the mean of that (theoretical) population have the same value as the regular population? H_0 says it does. H_1 says it's larger.

The test statistic is

$$z = \frac{(\bar{x}_1 - \bar{x}_2) - (\mu_1 - \mu_2)}{\sigma_{\bar{x}_1 - \bar{x}_2}} = \frac{(\bar{x}_1 - \bar{x}_2) - (\mu_1 - \mu_2)}{\sqrt{\dfrac{\sigma_1^2}{N_1} + \dfrac{\sigma_2^2}{N_2}}}$$

$$= \frac{(107 - 101.2)}{\sqrt{\dfrac{16^2}{25} + \dfrac{16^2}{25}}} = \frac{5.8}{4.53} = 1.28$$

With $\alpha = .05$, the critical value of z — the value that cuts off the upper 5 percent of the area under the standard normal distribution — is 1.645. (You can use the qnorm( ) function from Chapter 7 to verify this.) The calculated value of the test statistic is less than the critical value, so the decision is to not reject H_0. Figure 10-3 summarizes this.

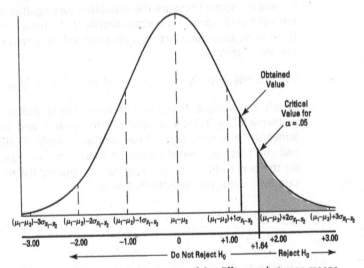

FIGURE 10-3: The sampling distribution of the difference between means, along with the critical value for $\alpha = .05$ and the obtained value of the test statistic in the IQ example.

Z-testing for two samples in R

As is the case for one-sample testing (explained in Chapter 9), base R provides no function for a two-sample z-test. If this function existed, you'd probably want it to work like this for the example:

```
> sample1 <-c(100,118,97,92,118,125,136,95,111)
> sample2 <-c(91,109,83,88,115,108,127,102,86)
> z.test2(sample1,sample2,15,15)
mean1 = 110.2222    mean2 = 101
standard error = 7.071068
z = 1.304
one-tailed probability = 0.096
two-tailed probability = 0.192
```

Because this function isn't available, I'll show you how to create one.

Begin with the function name and the arguments:

```
z.test2 = function(x,y,popsd1,popsd2){
```

The first two arguments are data vectors, and the second two are the population standard deviations. The left curly bracket indicates that subsequent statements are what occurs inside the function.

Next, you initialize a vector that will hold the one-tailed probability:

```
one.tail.p <- NULL
```

Then you calculate the standard error of the difference between means

```
std.error <- sqrt((popsd1^2/length(x) + popsd2^2/
  length(y)))
```

and then the (rounded) z-score

```
z.score <- round((mean(x)-mean(y))/std.error,3)
```

Finally, you calculate the rounded one-tailed probability:

```
one.tail.p <- round(pnorm(abs(z.score),lower.tail =
    FALSE),3)
```

The abs() function (absolute value) ensures that the appropriate calculation for a negative z-score.

Last but not least, a cat() (concatenate-and-print) statement displays the output:

```
cat(" mean1 =", mean(x)," ", "mean2 =", mean(y),
    "\n",
        "standard error =", std.error, "\n",
        "z =", z.score,"\n",
        "one-tailed probability =", one.tail.p,"\n",
        "two-tailed probability =", 2*one.tail.p )}
```

I use a cat() function like this for the one-sample case in Chapter 9. The right curly bracket closes off the function.

Here's the newly defined function:

```
z.test2 = function(x,y,popsd1,popsd2){
  one.tail.p <- NULL
  std.error <- sqrt((popsd1^2/length(x) + popsd2^2/
  length(y)))
  z.score <- round((mean(x)-mean(y))/std.error,3)
  one.tail.p <- round(pnorm(abs(z.score),lower.
  tail = FALSE),3)
  cat(" mean1 =", mean(x)," ", "mean2 =", mean(y),
  "\n",
        "standard error =", std.error, "\n",
        "z =", z.score,"\n",
        "one-tailed probability =", one.tail.p,"\n",
        "two-tailed probability =", 2*one.tail.p )}
```

t for Two

The example in the preceding section involves a situation you rarely encounter — known population variances. If you know a population's variance, you're likely to know the population mean. If you know the mean, you probably don't have to perform hypothesis tests about it.

Not knowing the variances takes the central limit theorem out of play. This means that you can't use the normal distribution as an approximation of the sampling distribution of the difference between means. Instead, you use the t-distribution, a family of distributions I introduce in Chapter 8 and apply to one-sample hypothesis testing in Chapter 9. The members of this family of distributions differ from one another in terms of a parameter called *degrees of freedom* (df). Think of df as the denominator of the variance estimate you use when you calculate a value of t as a test statistic. Another way to say "calculate a value of t as a test statistic" is "Perform a t-test."

Unknown population variances lead to two possibilities for hypothesis testing. One possibility is that although the variances are unknown, you have reason to assume they're equal. The other possibility is that you cannot assume they're equal. In the sections that follow, I discuss these possibilities.

Like Peas in a Pod: Equal Variances

When you don't know a population variance, you use the sample variance to estimate it. If you have two samples, you average (sort of) the two sample variances to arrive at the estimate.

REMEMBER

Putting sample variances together to estimate a population variance is called *pooling*. With two sample variances, here's how you do it:

$$s_p^{\ 2} = \frac{(N_1 - 1)s_1^2 + (N_2 - 1)s_2^2}{(N_1 - 1) + (N_2 - 1)}$$

In this formula, $s_p^{\ 2}$ stands for the pooled estimate. Notice that the denominator of this estimate is $(N_1 - 1) + (N_2 - 1)$. Is this the df? Absolutely!

The formula for calculating t is

$$t = \frac{(\bar{x}_1 - \bar{x}_2) - (\mu_1 - \mu_2)}{s_p \sqrt{\dfrac{1}{N_1} + \dfrac{1}{N_2}}}$$

On to an example. FarKlempt Robotics is trying to choose between two machines to produce a component for its new microrobot. Speed is of the essence, so the company has each machine produce ten copies of the component and times each production run. The hypotheses are

$H_0: \mu_1 - \mu_2 = 0$

$H_1: \mu_1 - \mu_2 \neq 0$

They set α at .05. This is a two-tailed test because they don't know in advance which machine might be faster.

Table 10-1 presents the data for the production times in minutes.

TABLE 10-1 Sample Statistics from the FarKlempt Machine Study

	Machine 1	Machine 2
Mean Production Time	23.00	20.00
Standard Deviation	2.71	2.79
Sample Size	10	10

The pooled estimate of σ^2 is

$$s_p^2 = \frac{(N_1 - 1)s_1^2 + (N_2 - 1)s_2^2}{(N_1 - 1) + (N_2 - 1)} = \frac{(10 - 1)(2.71)^2 + (10 - 1)(2.79)^2}{(10 - 1) + (10 - 1)}$$

$$= \frac{(9)(2.71)^2 + (9)(2.79)^2}{(9) + (9)} = \frac{66 + 70}{18} = 7.56$$

The estimate of σ is 2.75, the square root of 7.56.

The test statistic is

$$t = \frac{(\bar{x}_1 - \bar{x}_2) - (\mu_1 - \mu_2)}{s_p \sqrt{\frac{1}{N_1} + \frac{1}{N_2}}} = \frac{(23 - 20)}{2.75 \sqrt{\frac{1}{10} + \frac{1}{10}}} = \frac{3}{1.23} = 2.44$$

For this test statistic, df = 18, the denominator of the variance estimate. In a t-distribution with 18 df, the critical value is 2.10 for the right-side (upper) tail and –2.10 for the left-side (lower) tail. If you don't believe me, apply qt(). (See Chapter 9.) The calculated value of the test statistic is greater than 2.10, so the decision is to reject H_0. The data provide evidence that Machine 2 is significantly faster than Machine 1. (You can use the word *significant* whenever you reject H_0.)

t-Testing in R

Here are a couple of vectors for the sample data in the example in the preceding section:

```
machine1 <-c(24.58, 22.09, 23.70, 18.89, 22.02,
   28.71, 24.44, 20.91, 23.83, 20.83)
```

```
machine2 <- c(21.61, 19.06, 20.72, 15.77, 19,
   25.88, 21.48, 17.85, 20.86, 17.77)
```

R provides two ways for performing the t-test. Both involve t.test(), which I use in Chapters 8 and 9.

Working with two vectors

Here's how to test the hypotheses with two vectors and the equal variances assumption:

```
t.test(machine1,machine2,var.equal = TRUE,
   alternative="two.sided", mu=0)
```

The alternative=two.sided argument reflects the type of alternative hypothesis specified in the example, and the last argument indicates the hypothesized difference between means.

Running that function produces this output:

```
Two Sample t-test

data:    machine1 and machine2

t = 2.4396, df = 18, p-value = 0.02528
alternative hypothesis: true difference in means
   is not equal to 0
95 percent confidence interval:
 0.4164695 5.5835305
sample estimates:
mean of x mean of y
        23        20
```

The t-value and the low p-value indicate that you can reject the null hypothesis. Machine 2 is significantly faster than Machine 1.

Working with a data frame and a formula

The other way of carrying out this test is to create a data frame and then use a formula that looks like this:

```
prod.time ~ machine
```

The formula expresses the idea that production time depends on the machine you use. Although it's not necessary to do the test this way, it's a good idea to get accustomed to formulas. I use them quite a bit in later chapters.

The first thing to do is create a data frame in long format. First you create a vector for the 20 production times — machine1's times first and then machine2's:

```
prod.time <- c(machine1,machine2)
```

Next, you create a vector of the two machine names:

```
machine <-c("machine1","machine2")
```

Then you turn that vector into a vector of ten repetitions of "machine1" followed by ten repetitions of "machine2". It's a little tricky, but here's how:

```
machine <- rep(machine, times = c(10,10))
```

And the data frame is

```
FarKlempt.frame <-data.frame(machine,prod.time)
```

Its first six rows are

```
> head(FarKlempt.frame)
   machine prod.time
1 machine1    24.58
2 machine1    22.09
3 machine1    23.70
4 machine1    18.89
5 machine1    22.02
6 machine1    28.71
```

The t.test() function is then

```
with (FarKlempt.frame,t.test(prod.time ~ machine,
    var.equal = TRUE,
    alternative="two.sided",mu=0))
```

This produces the same output as the two-vector version, except for the first line which is

```
data:   prod.time by machine
```

Like p's and q's: Unequal variances

The case of unequal variances presents a challenge. As it happens, when variances are not equal, the t-distribution with $(N_1-1) + (N_2-1)$ degrees of freedom is not as close an approximation to the sampling distribution as statisticians would like.

Statisticians meet this challenge by reducing the degrees of freedom. To accomplish the reduction, they use a fairly involved formula that depends on the sample standard deviations and the sample sizes.

Because the variances aren't equal, a pooled estimate is not appropriate. So you calculate the t-test in a different way:

$$t = \frac{(\bar{x}_1 - \bar{x}_2) - (\mu_1 - \mu_2)}{\sqrt{\frac{s_1^2}{N_1} + \frac{s_2^2}{N_2}}}$$

You evaluate the test statistic against a member of the t-distribution family that has the reduced degrees of freedom.

Here's what t.test() produces for the FarKlempt example if I assume the variances are not equal:

```
with (FarKlempt.frame,t.test(prod.time ~ machine,
                             var.equal = FALSE,
                             alternative="two.
  sided",
                             mu=0))
```

```
Welch Two Sample t-test

data:  prod.time by machine
t = 2.4396, df = 17.985, p-value = 0.02529
alternative hypothesis:  true difference in means
   between group machine1 and group machine2 is not
   equal to 0

95 percent confidence interval:
 0.4163193 5.5836807
sample estimates:
mean in group machine1 mean in group machine2
                    23                     20
```

You can see the slight reduction in degrees of freedom. The variances are so close that little else changes.

A Matched Set: Hypothesis Testing for Paired Samples

In the hypothesis tests I describe so far, the samples are independent of one another. Choosing an individual for one sample has no bearing on the choice of an individual for the other.

Sometimes, the samples are matched. The most obvious case is when the same individual provides a score under each of two conditions — as in a before-after study. Suppose ten people participate in a weight-loss program. They weigh in before they start the program and again after one month on the program. The important data is the set of before-after differences. Table 10-2 shows the data:

TABLE 10-2 Data for the Weight-Loss Example

Person	Weight Before Program	Weight After One Month	Difference
1	198	194	4
2	201	203	-2
3	210	200	10
4	185	183	2
5	204	200	4
6	156	153	3
7	167	166	1
8	197	197	0
9	220	215	5
10	186	184	2
Mean			2.9
Standard Deviation			3.25

The idea is to think of these differences as a sample of scores and treat them as you would in a one-sample t-test (see Chapter 9).

You carry out a test on these hypotheses:

$$H_0: \mu_d \leq 0$$

$$H_1: \mu_d > 0$$

The d in the subscripts stands for "difference." Set $\alpha = .05$.

The formula for this kind of t-test is

$$t = \frac{\bar{d} - \mu_d}{s_{\bar{d}}}$$

In this formula, $\bar{d}$ is the mean of the differences. To find $s_{\bar{d}}$, you calculate the standard deviation of the differences and divide by the square root of the number of pairs:

$$s_{\bar{d}} = \frac{s}{\sqrt{N}}$$

The df is N-1 (where N is the number of pairs).

From Table 10-2,

$$t = \frac{\bar{d} - \mu_d}{s_d} = \frac{2.9}{\left(3.25 / \sqrt{10}\right)} = 2.82$$

With df = 9 (Number of pairs − 1), the critical value for $\alpha = .05$ is 1.83. (Use qt( ) to verify.) The calculated value exceeds this value, so the decision is to reject H_0.

Paired Sample t-testing in R

For paired sample t-tests, it's the same formula as for independent samples t-tests. As you'll see, you add an argument. Here's the data from Table 10-2:

```
before <-c(198,201,210,185,204,156,167,197,220,186)
after <- c(194,203,200,183,200,153,166,197,215,184)
```

And the t-test:

```
t.test(before,after,alternative = "greater",
    paired=TRUE)
```

That last argument, of course, specifies a paired-samples test. The default value for that one is FALSE.

Running that test yields

```
    Paired t-test

data:  before and after
t = 2.8241, df = 9, p-value = 0.009956
  true mean difference is greater than 0
95 percent confidence interval:
  1.017647      Inf
sample estimates:
 mean difference
                 2.9
```

Because of the very low p-value, you reject the null hypothesis.

Chapter **11**
Testing More Than Two Samples

S tatistics would be limited if you could only make inferences about one or two samples. In this chapter, I discuss the procedures for testing hypotheses about three or more samples. I show what to do when samples are independent of one another, and what to do when they're not. In both cases, I discuss what to do after you test the hypotheses. I also discuss R functions that do the work for you.

Testing More Than Two

Imagine this situation. Your company asks you to evaluate three different methods for training its employees to do a particular job. You randomly assign 30 employees to one of the three methods. Your plan is to train them, test them, tabulate the results, and make some conclusions. Before you can finish the study, three people leave the company — one from the Method 1 group and two from the Method 3 group.

Table 11-1 shows the data.

TABLE 11-1 Data from Three Training Methods

	Method 1	Method 2	Method 3
	95	83	68
	91	89	75
	89	85	79
	90	89	74
	99	81	75
	88	89	81
	96	90	73
	98	82	77
	95	84	
		80	
Mean	93.44	85.20	75.25
Variance	16.28	14.18	15.64

Do the three methods provide different results, or are they so similar that you can't distinguish among them? To decide, you have to carry out a hypothesis test:

$H_0: \mu_1 = \mu_2 = \mu_3$

$H_1:$ Not H_0

with $\alpha = .05$.

In this context, however, the idea is to think in terms of variances rather than means.

I'd like you to consider variance in a slightly different way. The formula for estimating population variance, remember, is

$$s^2 = \frac{\sum(x - \bar{x})^2}{N - 1}$$

Because the variance is almost a mean of squared deviations from the mean, statisticians also refer to it as *mean square*. In a way, that's an unfortunate nickname: It leaves out "deviation from the mean," but there you have it.

The numerator of the variance — excuse me, mean square — is the sum of squared deviations from the mean. This leads to another nickname, *sum of squares*. The denominator, as I say in Chapter 9, is *degrees of freedom* (df). So, the slightly different way to think of variance is

$$\text{Mean Square} = \frac{\text{Sum of Squares}}{\text{df}}$$

You can abbreviate this as

$$MS = \frac{SS}{df}$$

One important step is to find the mean squares hiding in the data. Another is to understand that you use these mean squares to estimate the variances of the populations that produced these samples. In this case, assume that those variances are equal, so you're really estimating one variance. The final step is to understand that you use these estimates to test the hypotheses I show you at the beginning of the chapter.

Three different mean squares are inside the data in Table 11-1. Start with the whole set of 27 scores, forgetting for the moment that they're divided into three groups. Suppose that you want to use those 27 scores to calculate an estimate of the population variance. (A dicey idea, but humor me.) The mean of those 27 scores is 85. I'll call that mean the *grand mean* because it's the average of everything.

So the mean square would be

$$\frac{(95-85)^2 + (91-85)^2 + \ldots + (73-85)^2 + (77-85)^2}{(27-1)} = 68.08$$

The denominator has 26 (27 − 1) degrees of freedom. I refer to that variance as the *total variance*, or in the new way of thinking about this, the MS_{Total}. It's often abbreviated as MS_T.

Here's another variance to consider. In Chapter 10, I describe the *t*-test for two samples with equal variances. For that test, you put together the two sample variances to create a *pooled* estimate of the population variance. The data in Table 11-1 provides three sample variances for a pooled estimate: 16.28, 14.18, and 15.64. Assuming that these numbers represent equal population variances, the pooled estimate is

$$s_p^2 = \frac{(N_1-1)s_1^2 + (N_2-1)s_2^2 + (N_3-1)s_3^2}{(N_1-1)+(N_2-1)+(N_3-1)}$$

$$= \frac{(9-1)(16.28)+(10-1)(14.18)+(8-1)(15.64)}{(9-1)+(10-1)+(8-1)} = 15.31$$

Because this pooled estimate comes from the variance within the groups, it's called MS_{Within}, or MS_W.

One more mean square to go — the variance of the sample means around the grand mean. In this example, that means the variance in these numbers 93.44, 85.20, and 75.25 — sort of. I say "sort of" because these are means, not scores. When you deal with means, you have to take into account the number of scores that produced each mean. To do that, you multiply each squared deviation by the number of scores in that sample.

So this variance is

$$\frac{(9)(93.44-85)^2 + (10)(85.20-85)^2 + (8)(75.25-85)^2}{3-1} = 701.34$$

The df for this variance is 2 (the number of samples − 1).

Statisticians, not known for their crispness of usage, refer to this as the variance *between* sample means. (*Among* is the correct word when you're talking about more than two items.) This variance is known as $MS_{Between}$, or MS_B.

So you now have three estimates of population variance: MS_T, MS_W, and MS_B. What do you do with them?

Remember that the original objective is to test a hypothesis about three means. According to H_0, any differences you see among the three sample means are due strictly to chance. The implication is that the variance among those means is the same as the variance of any three numbers selected at random from the population.

If you could somehow compare the variance among the means (that's MS_B, remember) with the population variance, you could see if that holds up. If only you had an estimate of the population variance that's independent of the differences among the groups, you'd be in business.

Ah . . . but you do have that estimate. You have MS_W, an estimate based on pooling the variances within the samples. Assuming that those variances represent equal population variances, this is a solid estimate. In this example, it's based on 24 degrees of freedom.

The reasoning now becomes: If MS_B is about the same as MS_W, you have evidence consistent with H_0. If MS_B is significantly larger than MS_W, you have evidence that's inconsistent with H_0. In effect, you transform these hypotheses

$H_0: \mu_1 = \mu_2 = \mu_3$

$H_1:$ Not H_0

into these

$H_0: \sigma_B^2 \leq \sigma_W^2$

$H_1: \sigma_B^2 > \sigma_W^2$

In effect, you perform a test of the difference between two variances.

The test is called the F-test. To perform this test, you divide one variance by the other. You evaluate the result against a family of distributions called the F-distribution. Because two variances are involved, two values for degrees of freedom define each member of the family.

For this example, F has df = 2 (for the MS_B) and df = 24 (for the MS_W). For our purposes, it's the distribution of possible F values if H_0 is true.

The test statistic for the example is

$$F = \frac{701.34}{15.31} = 45.82$$

What proportion of area does this value cut off in the upper tail of the F-distribution? It's way less than .05.

This means that it's highly unlikely that differences among the means are due to chance. It means that you reject H_0.

This whole procedure for testing more than two samples is called the *analysis of variance*, often abbreviated as ANOVA. In the context of ANOVA, the denominator of an F-ratio has the generic name *error term*. The independent variable is sometimes called a *factor*. So this is a single-factor or (1-factor) ANOVA.

In this example, the factor is Training Method. Each instance of the independent variable is called a *level*. The independent variable in this example has three levels.

More complex studies have more than one factor, and each factor can have many levels.

In an ANOVA, it's always the case that

$$df_B + df_W = df_T$$

Also:

$$SS_B + SS_W = SS_T$$

In fact, statisticians who work with the analysis of variance speak of partitioning (read "breaking down into non-overlapping pieces") the SS_T into one portion for the SS_B and another for the SS_W, and partitioning the df_T into one amount for the df_B and another for the df_W.

ANOVA in R

The R function for ANOVA is aov( ). Here's how it looks generically:

```
aov(Dependent_variable ~ Independent_variable,
    data)
```

In the example, the scores are the dependent variable and the method is the independent variable. So you need a 2-column data frame with *Method* in the first column and *Score* in the second. (This is equivalent to "long-form" data format.)

Start with a vector for each column in Table 11-1:

```
method1.scores <- c(95,91,89,90,99,88,96,98,95)
method2.scores <- c(83,89,85,89,81,89,90,82,84,80)
method3.scores <- c(68,75,79,74,75,81,73,77)
```

Then create a single vector that consists of all these scores:

```
Score <- c(method1.scores, method2.scores, method3.
  scores)
```

Next, create a vector consisting of the names of the methods, matched up against the scores. In other words, this vector has to consist of "method1" repeated nine times, followed by "method2" repeated ten times, followed by "method3" repeated eight times:

```
Method <- rep(c("method1", "method2", "method3"),
  times=c(length(method1.scores), length(method2.
  scores), length(method3.scores)))
```

At this point, I turn Method into a factor. (It's helpful for what we'll do after the analysis):

```
Method <- factor(Method)
```

The data frame is then

```
Training.frame <- data.frame(Method,Score)
```

And the ANOVA is

```
analysis <-aov(Score ~ Method,data = Training.
  frame)
```

For a table of the analysis, use summary().

```
> summary(analysis)
            Df Sum Sq Mean Sq F value   Pr(>F)
Method       2 1402.7   701.3   45.82 6.38e-09 ***
Residuals   24  367.3    15.3
---
Signif. codes: 0 '***' 0.001 '**' 0.01 '*' 0.05
  '.' 0.1 ' ' 1
```

The first column consists of Method and Residuals, which map onto Between and Within from the preceding section. A *residual*, in this context, is a score's deviation from its group mean. (I have more to say about residuals in Chapter 12.) The next columns provide degrees of freedom, SS, MS, F, and p.

The high value of F and the tiny value of p (listed here as $\mathrm{Pr(>F)}$) tell you to reject the null hypothesis. The significance codes tell you that F is so high that you can reject the null hypothesis even if α is .0001.

After the ANOVA

The ANOVA enables you to decide whether or not to reject H_0. After you decide to reject, then what? All you can say is that somewhere within the set of means, something is different from something else. The analysis doesn't specify what those "somethings" are.

In order to get more specific, you have to do some further tests. Not only that, you have to plan those tests in advance of carrying out the ANOVA.

These post-ANOVA tests are called *planned comparisons.* Some statisticians refer to them as *a priori tests* or *contrasts*. I illustrate by following through with the example. Suppose that before you gathered the data, you had reason to believe that Method 2 would result in higher scores than Method 3 and that Method 1 would result in higher scores than Method 2 and Method 3 averaged together. In that case, you plan in advance to compare the means of those samples in the event your ANOVA-based decision is to reject H_0.

As I mention earlier, the overall analysis partitions the SS_T into the SS_B and the SS_W, and the df_T into the df_B and the df_W. Planned comparisons further partition the SS_B and the df_B. Each contrast (remember, that's another name for "planned comparison") has its own SS along with 1 df. I refer to Method 2 versus Method 3 as *Contrast1* and Method 1 versus the average of Method 2 and 3 as *Contrast2*. For this example,

$$SS_{Contrast1} + SS_{Contrast2} = SS_B$$

and

$$df_{Contrast1} + df_{Contrast2} = df_B$$

Because each SS has 1 df, it's equal to its corresponding MS. Dividing the SS for the contrast by MS_w yields an F-ratio for the contrast. The F has df=1 and df_w. If that F cuts off less than .05 in the upper tail of its F-distribution, reject the null hypothesis for that contrast (and you can refer to the contrast as "statistically significant").

It's possible to set up a contrast between two means as an expression that involves all three of the sample means. For example, to compare Method 2 versus Method 3, I can write the difference between them as

$$(0)\bar{x}_1 + (+1)\bar{x}_2 + (-1)\bar{x}_3$$

The 0, +1, and −1 are *comparison coefficients*. I refer to them, in a general way, as c_1, c_2, and c_3. To compare Method 1 versus the average of Method 2 and Method 3, it's

$$(+2)\bar{x}_1 + (-1)\bar{x}_2 + (-1)\bar{x}_3$$

The important point is that the coefficients add up to 0. How do you use the comparison coefficients and the means to calculate a SS for a contrast? For this example, here's $SS_{Contrast1}$:

$$SS_{Contrast1} = \frac{((0)(93.44) + (+1)(85.20) + (-1)(75.25))^2}{\frac{(0)^2}{9} + \frac{(+1)^2}{10} + \frac{(-1)^2}{8}} = 358.5$$

And here's $SS_{Contrast2}$:

$$SS_{Contrast2} = \frac{((+2)(93.44) + (-1)(85.20) + (-1)(75.25))^2}{\frac{(2)^2}{9} + \frac{(-1)^2}{10} + \frac{(-1)^2}{8}} = 1044.2$$

In general, the formula is

$$SS_{Contrast} = \frac{\sum c_j \bar{x}_j}{\sum \left(\frac{c_j^2}{n_j} \right)}$$

in which the j subscript stands for "level of the independent variable" (for Method 1, $j=1$, for example).

For Contrast 1

$$F_{1,24} = \frac{SS_{Contrast1}}{MS_{Within}} = \frac{358.5}{15.3} = 23.42$$

and for Contrast 2

$$F_{1,24} = \frac{SS_{Contrast2}}{MS_{Within}} = \frac{1044.2}{15.3} = 68.22$$

Are these contrasts significant? Yes, they are — meaning that Method 2 yields significantly higher learning than Method 3, and that Method 1 results in significantly higher learning than the average of Methods 2 and 3. You can use pf( ) to verify (or wait until the upcoming subsection "Contrasts in R").

Another word about contrasts

Earlier, I say that the important thing about a contrast is that its coefficients add up to 0. Another important thing is the relationship between the coefficients in a set of contrasts. In the two contrasts I show you, the sum of the products of corresponding coefficients is 0:

$$((0)(+2))+((+1)(-1))+((-1)(-1)) = 0$$

When this happens, the contrasts are *orthogonal*. This means they have no overlapping information. It doesn't mean that other contrasts aren't possible. It's just that other contrasts would be part of a different set (or sets) of orthogonal contrasts.

Contrasts in R

The objective here is to create a table of the ANOVA that shows the contrasts partitioning the SS_B and will show the associated F-ratios and p-values. It will look like this:

```
                       Df Sum Sq Mean Sq F value
     Pr(>F)
Method                  2 1402.7   701.3   45.82
     6.38e-09 ***
Method: 2 vs 3          1  358.5   358.5   23.42
     6.24e-05 ***
Method: 1 vs 2 & 3      1 1044.2  1044.2   68.22
     1.78e-08 ***
```

```
Residuals              24  367.3    15.3
---
Signif. codes: 0 '***' 0.001 '**' 0.01 '*' 0.05
  '.' 0.1 ' ' 1
```

Remember when I turned Method into a factor earlier? Here's where that becomes important.

To set up for the contrasts, you first create a matrix of the coefficients in the set of orthogonal contrasts:

```
contrasts(Training.frame$Method) <-
    matrix(c(0,1,-1,2,-1,-1),3,2)
```

On the left, the term inside the parentheses specifies what to contrast — the levels of the independent variable Method in the Training.frame. On the right, the matrix() function creates a matrix with the coefficients in the columns:

```
> contrasts(Training.frame$Method)
          [,1] [,2]
method1     0    2
method2     1   -1
method3    -1   -1
```

Next, you run the analysis of variance, but this time with a contrasts argument, which, as you'll see, is a bit tricky.

```
Anova.w.Contrasts <-aov(Score ~ Method,
    data=Training.frame,
  contrasts = list(Method=(contrasts(Training.frame
    $Method)))
```

How do you create the table at the beginning of this subsection? With a summary() statement that adds a little twist:

```
summary(Anova.w.Contrasts,split=list(Method=list
  ("2 vs 3"= 1,
  "1 vs 2 & 3" = 2)))
```

The little twist (a little "split," actually) is in the second argument. The goal is to partition Method into two pieces — one that corresponds to the first contrast and one that corresponds to the second. You do that with split, which divides a list into the indicated number of components and reassembles the list with a name assigned to each component. In this case, the list is Method split into a list with two components. The name of each component corresponds to what's in the contrast.

Running that summary statement produces the table at the top of this subsection.

Another Kind of Hypothesis, Another Kind of Test

The preceding ANOVA works with independent samples. As Chapter 10 explains, sometimes you work with matched samples. For example, sometimes a person provides data in a number of different conditions. In this section, I introduce the ANOVA you use when you have more than two matched samples. This type of ANOVA is called *repeated measures*.

To show how this works, I extend the example from Chapter 10. In that example, ten men participate in a weight-loss program. Table 11-2 shows their data over a three-month period.

TABLE 11-2 Data for the Weight-Loss Example

Person	Before	One Month	Two Months	Three Months	Mean
Al	198	194	191	188	192.75
Bill	201	203	200	196	200.00
Charlie	210	200	192	188	197.50
Dan	185	183	180	178	181.50
Ed	204	200	195	191	197.50
Fred	156	153	150	145	151.00
Gary	167	166	167	166	166.50

Person	Before	One Month	Two Months	Three Months	Mean
Harry	197	197	195	192	195.25
Irv	220	215	209	205	212.25
Jon	186	184	179	175	181.00
Mean	**192.4**	**189.5**	**185.8**	**182.4**	**187.525**

Is the program effective? This question calls for a hypothesis test:

$H_0: \mu_{Before} = \mu_1 = \mu_2 = \mu_3$

$H_1:$ Not H_0

Once again, you set $\alpha = .05$

To set the stage for the repeated measures ANOVA in R, put the columns of Table 11-2 into vectors:

```
Person <-c("Al", "Bill", "Charlie", "Dan", "Ed",
   "Fred", "Gary","Harry","Irv","Jon")
Before <- c(198,201,210,185,204,156,167,197,220,186)
OneMonth <- c(194,203,200,183,200,153,166,197,
   215,184)
TwoMonths <- c(191,200,192,180,195,150,167,195,
   209,179)
ThreeMonths <- c(188,196,188,178,191,145,166,192,
   205,175)
```

Then create a data frame:

```
Weight.frame <- data.frame(Person, Before,
   OneMonth, TwoMonths, ThreeMonths)
```

The data frame looks like this:

```
> Weight.frame
    Person Before OneMonth TwoMonths ThreeMonths
1       Al    198      194       191         188
2     Bill    201      203       200         196
3  Charlie    210      200       192         188
4      Dan    185      183       180         178
```

5	Ed	204	200	195	191
6	Fred	156	153	150	145
7	Gary	167	166	167	166
8	Harry	197	197	195	192
9	Irv	220	215	209	205
10	Jon	186	184	179	175

It's in wide format, and you have to reshape it. Install the reshape2 package, and after it's installed, select the check box next to reshape2 on the Packages tab. Then melt the data into long format:

```
Weight.frame.melt <- melt(Weight.frame,id="Person")
```

Next, assign column names to the melted data frame:

```
colnames(Weight.frame.melt) = c("Person","Time",
    "Weight")
```

And now, the first six rows of the new data frame are

```
> head(Weight.frame.melt)
   Person   Time Weight
1       Al Before    198
2     Bill Before    201
3  Charlie Before    210
4      Dan Before    185
5       Ed Before    204
6     Fred Before    156
```

In addition to Person, you now have Time as an independent variable.

The formula for the analysis is a bit different than for the independent groups ANOVA:

```
rm.anova <- aov(Weight ~ Time + Error
    (Person/Time),
               data = Weight.frame.melt)
```

Weight depends on Time and also on Person, and each Person experiences all levels of Time. The effect of Time — decreasing body weight over the four levels of Time — is evident within each Person. (It's easier to see that in the wide format than in the long.)

And now for the table

```
> summary(rm.anova)

Error: Person
           Df Sum Sq Mean Sq F value Pr(>F)
Residuals   9  11632    1292

Error: Person:Time
           Df Sum Sq Mean Sq F value  Pr(>F)
Time        3  569.1  189.69   24.48 7.3e-08 ***
Residuals  27  209.2    7.75
---
Signif. codes: 0 '***' 0.001 '**' 0.01 '*' 0.05
    '.' 0.1 ' ' 1
```

Now the analysis shows the significant effect of Time.

Getting Trendy

In situations like the one in the weight-loss example, you have an independent variable that's quantitative — its levels are numbers (0 months, 1 month, 2 months, 3 months). Not only that, but in this case, the intervals are equal.

With this kind of independent variable, it's often a good idea to look for patterns in the data rather than just plan comparisons among means.

Trend analysis is the statistical procedure that examines patterns (also known as *trends*). The objective is to see whether the pattern contributes to the significant differences among the means.

Take a look at the means in the bottom row of Table 11-2. They show a decrease from one month to the next. This is an example of a *linear trend* (a trend that has just one direction). A trend can also be nonlinear (in which the means appear to fall along a curve). The two nonlinear types of curves for four means are called *quadratic* and *cubic*. If the means show a quadratic trend, they align in a pattern that shows one change of direction.

If the means show a cubic trend, they align in a pattern that shows two changes of direction.

The three components are orthogonal, so

$$SS_{Linear} + SS_{Quadratic} + SS_{Cubic} = SS_{Time}$$

and

$$df_{Linear} + df_{Quadratic} + df_{Cubic} = df_{Time}$$

To analyze a trend, you use comparison coefficients — those numbers you use in contrasts. You use them in a slightly different way than you did before. The formula for computing a SS for a trend component is

$$SS_{Component} = \frac{N\left(\sum c\bar{x}\right)^2}{\sum c^2}$$

In this formula, N is the number of people and c represents the coefficients.

The comparison coefficients are different for different numbers of samples. For four samples, the linear coefficients are −3, −1, 1, and 3. The quadratic coefficients are 1, −1, −1, and 1. The cubic coefficients are −1, 3, −3, and 1.

TIP The easiest way to get the coefficients is to look them up in a stat textbook or on the Internet!

How do you carry out this analysis in R? Read on.

Trend Analysis in R

I treat this analysis pretty much the same way as contrasts for the independent samples example. I begin by creating a matrix of the coefficients for the three trend components:

```
contrasts(Weight.frame.melt$Time) <-
    matrix(c(-3,-1,1,3,1,-1, -1,1,-1,3,-3,1), 4, 3)
```

Then I run the ANOVA, adding the contrasts argument:

```
rm.anova <- aov(Weight ~ Time +
  Error(factor(Person)/Time), data=Weight.frame.
  melt,
contrasts = list(Time = contrasts(Weight.frame.
  melt$Time)))
```

Finally, I apply summary( ) (including the split of Time into three components) to print the table of the analysis:

```
summary(rm.anova,split=list(Time=list("Linear" =1,
  "Quadratic"=2,"Cubic" =3)))
```

Running this statement produces this table:

```
Error: factor(Person)
          Df Sum Sq Mean Sq F value Pr(>F)
Residuals  9  11632    1292


Error: factor(Person):Time
                Df Sum Sq Mean Sq F value
  Pr(>F)
Time             3  569.1   189.7  24.485
  7.30e-08 ***
  Time: Linear    1  567.8   567.8  73.297
  3.56e-09 ***
  Time: Quadratic 1    0.6     0.6   0.081
  0.779
  Time: Cubic     1    0.6     0.6   0.078
  0.782
Residuals        27  209.2     7.7
---
Signif. codes: 0 '***' 0.001 '**' 0.01 '*' 0.05
  '.' 0.1 ' ' 1
```

You can see the overwhelming linearity of the trend — just as we would expect from the way the means in the bottom row of Table 11-2 show a steady decrease from month to month.

Chapter **12**

Linear Regression

O ne of the main things you do when you work with statistics is make predictions. The idea is to use data from one or more variables to predict the value of another variable. To do this, you have to understand how to summarize relationships among variables, and to test hypotheses about those relationships.

In this chapter, I introduce *regression*, a statistical way to do just that. Regression also enables you to use the details of relationships to make predictions.

The Plot of Scatter

FarMisht Consulting, Inc., is a consulting firm with a wide range of specialties. It receives numerous applications from people interested in becoming FarMisht consultants. Accordingly, FarMisht Human Resources has to be able to predict which applicants will succeed and which ones will not. They've developed a Performance measure that they use to assess their current employees. The scale is 0–100, where 100 indicates top performance.

What's the best prediction for a new applicant? Without knowing anything about an applicant, and knowing only their own employees' Performance scores, the answer is clear: It's the average Performance score among their employees. Regardless of who the applicant is, that's all the Human Resources team can say if its knowledge is limited to Performance scores.

With more knowledge about the employees and about the applicants, a more accurate prediction becomes possible. For example, if FarMisht develops an Aptitude test and assesses its employees, Human Resources can match up every employee's Performance score with their Aptitude score and see whether the two pieces of data are somehow related. If they are, an applicant can take the FarMisht aptitude test, and Human Resources can use that score (and the relationship between Aptitude and Performance) to help make a prediction.

Figure 12-1 shows the Aptitude-Performance matchup in a graphical way. Because the points are scattered, it's called a *scatterplot*. By convention, the vertical axis (the *y-axis*) represents what you're trying to predict. That's also called the *dependent variable*, or the *y-variable*. In this case, that's Performance. Also by convention, the horizontal axis (the *x-axis*) represents what you're using to make your prediction. That's also called the *independent variable*, or *x-variable*. Here, that's Aptitude.

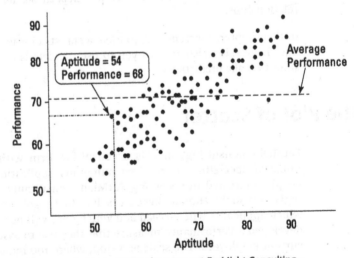

FIGURE 12-1: Aptitude and Performance at FarMisht Consulting.

Each point in the graph represents an individual's Performance and Aptitude. In a scatterplot for a real-life corporation, you'd see many more points than I show here. The general tendency of the set of points seems to be that high Aptitude scores are associated with high Performance scores and that low Aptitude scores are associated with low Performance scores.

I've singled out one of the points. It shows a FarMisht employee with an Aptitude score of 54 and a Performance score of 58. I also show the average Performance score, to give you a sense that knowing the Aptitude-Performance relationship provides an advantage over knowing only the mean.

How do you make that advantage work for you? You start by summarizing the relationship between Aptitude and Performance. In a plot like this, the summary is a line through the points. How and where do you draw the line?

Regression: What a Line!

Intuitively, the "best fitting" line ought to be the one that passes through the maximum number of points and isn't too far away from the points it doesn't pass through. For statisticians, that line has a special property: If you draw that line through the scatterplot, then draw distances (in the vertical direction) between the points and the line and then square those distances and add them up, the sum of the squared distances is a minimum.

Statisticians call this line the *regression line*, and they indicate it as

$$y' = a + bx$$

in which a is the intercept (where the line intersects with the y-axis) and b is the slope (how slanted the line is).

Each y' is a point on the line. It represents the best prediction of y for a given value of x.

To figure out exactly where this line is, you calculate its slope and its intercept. For a regression line, the slope and intercept are called *regression coefficients*.

The formulas for the regression coefficients are straightforward. For the slope, the formula is

$$b = \frac{\sum(x - \bar{x})(y - \bar{y})}{\sum(x - \bar{x})^2}$$

The intercept formula is

$$a = \bar{y} - b\bar{x}$$

I illustrate with an example. To keep the numbers manageable and comprehensible, I use a small sample instead of the hundreds (or perhaps thousands) of employees you'd find in a scatterplot for a corporation. Table 12-1 shows a sample of data from 16 FarMisht consultants.

TABLE 12-1 Aptitude Scores and Performance Scores for 16 FarMisht Consultants

Consultant	Aptitude	Performance
1	45	56
2	81	74
3	65	56
4	87	81
5	68	75
6	91	84
7	77	68
8	61	52
9	55	57
10	66	82
11	82	73
12	93	90
13	76	67
14	83	79

Consultant	Aptitude	Performance
15	61	70
16	74	66
Mean	72.81	70.63
Variance	181.63	126.65

For this set of data, the slope of the regression line is

$$b = \frac{(45-72.81)(56-70.63)+(81-72.81)(74-70.63)+\ldots}{(45-72.81)^2+(81-72.81)^2+\ldots+(74-72.81)^2}$$
$$= 0.654$$

The intercept is

$$a = \bar{y} - b\bar{x} = 70.63 - 0.654(72.81) = 23.03$$

So the equation of the best-fitting line through these 16 points is

$$y' = 23.03 + 0.654x$$

Or, in terms of Performance and Aptitude, it's

Predicted Performance = $23.03 + 0.654($*Aptitude*$)$

Using regression for forecasting

Based on this sample and this regression line, you can take an applicant's Aptitude score — say, 85 — and predict the applicant's Performance:

Predicted Performance = $23.03 + 0.654(85) = 78.59$

Without this regression line, the only prediction is the mean Performance, 70.63.

Variation around the regression line

In Chapter 5, I describe how the mean doesn't tell the whole story about a set of data. You have to show how the scores vary around the mean. For that reason, I introduce the variance and standard deviation.

You have a similar situation here. To get the full picture of the relationship in a scatterplot, you have to show how the scores vary around the regression line. Here, I introduce the *residual variance* and *standard error of estimate*, which are analogous to the variance and the standard deviation.

The residual variance is sort of an average of the squared deviations of the observed y-values around the predicted y-values. Each deviation of a data point from a predicted point $(y - y')$ is called a *residual*; hence, the name. The formula is

$$s_{yx}^2 = \frac{\sum(y - y')^2}{N - 2}$$

I say "sort of" because the denominator is $N-2$ rather than N. Telling you the reason for the -2 is beyond the scope of this discussion. As I mention earlier, the denominator of a variance estimate is *degrees of freedom* (df), and that concept comes in handy in a little while.

The standard error of estimate is

$$s_{yx} = \sqrt{s_{yx}^2} = \sqrt{\frac{\sum(y - y')^2}{N - 2}}$$

To show you how the residual error and the standard error of estimate play out for the data in the example, here's Table 12-2. This table extends Table 12-1 by showing the predicted Performance score for each given Aptitude score:

As the table shows, sometimes the predicted Performance score is pretty close, and sometimes it's not.

TABLE 12-2 **Aptitude Scores, Performance Scores, and Predicted Performance Scores for 16 FarMisht Consultants**

Consultant	Aptitude	Performance	Predicted Performance
1	45	56	52.44
2	81	74	75.98
3	65	56	65.52
4	87	81	79.90

Consultant	Aptitude	Performance	Predicted Performance
5	68	75	67.48
6	91	84	82.51
7	77	68	73.36
8	61	52	62.90
9	55	57	58.98
10	66	82	66.17
11	82	73	76.63
12	93	90	83.82
13	76	67	72.71
14	83	79	77.28
15	61	70	62.90
16	74	66	71.40
Mean	**72.81**	**70.63**	
Variance	**181.63**	**126.65**	

For these data, the residual variance is

$$s_{yx}^2 = \frac{\sum (y - y')^2}{N-2} = \frac{(56 - 52.44)^2 + (74 - 75.98)^2 + \dots + (66 - 71.40)^2}{16 - 2}$$

$$= \frac{735.65}{14} = 52.54$$

The standard error of estimate is

$$s_{yx} = \sqrt{s_{yx}^2} = \sqrt{52.54} = 7.25$$

If the residual variance and the standard error of estimate are small, the regression line is a good fit to the data in the scatterplot. If the residual variance and the standard error of estimate are large, the regression line is a poor fit.

What's "small"? What's "large"? What's a "good" fit?

Keep reading.

Testing Hypotheses about Regression

The objective is to decide whether or not the regression line really does represent a relationship between the variables. It's possible that what looks like a relationship is just due to chance and the equation of the regression line doesn't mean anything (because the amount of error is overwhelming) — or it's possible that the variables are strongly related. (Another possibility is that they're related in a nonlinear way, but that's beyond our scope.)

These possibilities are testable, and you set up hypotheses to test them:

H_0: No real relationship

H_1: Not H_0

Although those hypotheses make nice light reading, they don't set up a statistical test. To set up the test, you have to consider the variances. To consider the variances, you start with the deviations. Figure 12-2 focuses on one point in a scatterplot and its deviation from the regression line (the residual) and from the mean of the y-variable. It also shows the deviation between the regression line and the mean.

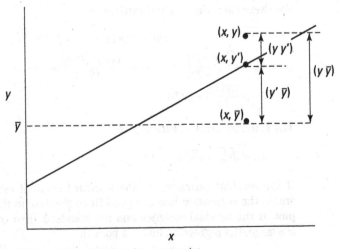

FIGURE 12-2: The deviations in a scatterplot.

As the figure shows, the distance between the point and the regression line and the distance between the regression line and the mean add up to the distance between the point and the mean:

$$(y - y') + (y' - \bar{y}) = (y - \bar{y})$$

This sets the stage for some other important relationships.

Start by squaring each deviation. That gives you $(y - y')^2$, $(y' - \bar{y})^2$, and $(y - \bar{y})^2$. If you add up each of the squared deviations throughout the scatterplot, you have three sums. The first one is

$$\sum (y - y')^2$$

You just saw this one. That's the numerator for the residual variance. It represents the variability around the regression line — the "error" I mention earlier. In the terminology of Chapter 11, the numerator of a variance is called a Sum of Squares, or SS. So this is $SS_{Residual}$.

The second one is

$$\sum (y' - \bar{y})^2$$

This one is new. The deviation $(y' - \bar{y})$ represents the gain in prediction due to using the regression line rather than the mean. The sum reflects this gain and is called $SS_{Regression}$.

The third one is

$$\sum (y - \bar{y})^2$$

I show you this one in Chapter 5 — although I use x rather than y. That's the numerator of the variance of y. In Chapter 11 terms, it's the numerator of *total variance*. This one is SS_{Total}.

This relationship holds among these three sums:

$$SS_{Residual} + SS_{Regression} = SS_{Total}$$

Each one is associated with a value for degrees of freedom — the denominator of a variance estimate. As I point out in the preceding section, the denominator for $SS_{Residual}$ is $N-2$. The df for SS_{Total} is $N-1$. (See Chapters 5 and 11.) As with the SS, the degrees of freedom add up:

$$df_{Residual} + df_{Regression} = df_{Total}$$

This leaves one degree of freedom for Regression.

Where is this all headed, and what does it have to do with hypothesis testing? Well, since you asked, you get variance estimates by dividing SS by df. Each variance estimate is called a *mean square*, abbreviated MS (again, see Chapter 11):

$$MS_{Regression} = \frac{SS_{Regression}}{df_{Regression}}$$

$$MS_{Residual} = \frac{SS_{Residual}}{df_{Residual}}$$

$$MS_{Total} = \frac{SS_{Total}}{df_{Total}}$$

Now for the hypothesis part. If H_0 is true and what looks like a relationship between x and y is really no big deal, the piece that represents the gain in prediction because of the regression line ($MS_{Regression}$) should be no greater than the variability around the regression line ($MS_{Residual}$). If H_0 is not true, and the gain in prediction is substantial, then $MS_{Regression}$ should be a lot bigger than $MS_{Residual}$.

So the hypotheses now set up as

$$H_0: \sigma^2_{Regression} \leq \sigma^2_{Residual}$$

$$H_1: \sigma^2_{Regression} > \sigma^2_{Residual}$$

These are hypotheses you can test. How? To test a hypothesis about two variances, you use an F test (as in ANOVA in Chapter 11). The test statistic here is

$$MS_{Total} = \frac{SS_{Total}}{df_{Total}}$$

To show you how it all works, I apply the formulas to the FarMisht example. The $MS_{Residual}$ is the same as s_{yx}^2 from the preceding section, and that value is 52.54. The $MS_{Regression}$ is

$$MS_{Regression} = \frac{(59.64 - 70.63)^2 + (71.40 - 70.63)^2 + \ldots + (66.17 - 70.63)^2}{1} = 1164.1$$

This sets up the F:

$$F = \frac{MS_{Regression}}{MS_{Residual}} = \frac{1164.1}{52.55} = 22.15$$

With 1 and 14 df and $\alpha = .05$, the critical value of F is 4.60. (Use `qf()` to verify.) The calculated F is greater than the critical F, so the decision is to reject H_0. That means the regression line provides a good fit to the data in the sample.

Linear Regression in R

Time to see how R handles linear regression. To start the analysis for this example, create a vector for the Aptitude scores and another for the Performance scores:

```
Aptitude <- c(45, 81, 65, 87, 68, 91, 77, 61, 55,
   66, 82, 93, 76, 83, 61, 74)
Performance <- c(56, 74, 56, 81, 75, 84, 68, 52,
   57, 82, 73, 90, 67, 79, 70, 66)
```

Then use the two vectors to create a data frame

```
FarMisht.frame <- data.frame(Aptitude,Performance)
```

The `lm()` (linear model) function performs the analysis:

```
FM.reg <-lm(Performance ~ Aptitude, data=FarMisht.
   frame)
```

As always, the tilde (~) operator signifies "depends on," so this is a perfect example of a dependent variable and an independent variable.

Applying `summary()` to `FM.reg` produces the regression information:

```
> summary(FM.reg)

Call:
lm(formula = Performance ~ Aptitude, data
   = FarMisht.frame)
```

```
Residuals:
     Min      1Q    Median      3Q      Max
 -10.9036  -5.3720  -0.4379   4.2111  15.8281

Coefficients:
            Estimate Std. Error t value Pr(>|t|)
(Intercept)  23.0299    10.2732   2.242 0.041697 *
Aptitude      0.6537     0.1389   4.707 0.000337
   ***
---
Signif. codes: 0 '***' 0.001 '**' 0.01 '*' 0.05
   '.' 0.1 ' ' 1

Residual standard error: 7.249 on 14 degrees of
   freedom
Multiple R-squared:  0.6128,   Adjusted R-squared:
   0.5851
F-statistic: 22.15 on 1 and 14 DF,  p-value:
   0.0003368
```

The first couple of lines provide summary information about the residuals. The coefficients table shows the intercept and slope of the regression line. If you divide each number in the Estimate column by the adjoining number in the Std. Error column, you get the number in the t value column. These t-values are significance tests for the intercept and the slope. The extremely low p-values indicate rejection of the null hypothesis (that a coefficient = 0) for each coefficient.

The bottom part of the output shows the info on how well the line fits the scatterplot, starting with the standard error of the residual. For our purposes, the bottom line is the bottom line: The F-statistic corresponds to the F-ratio I show you earlier. Its high value and low associated p-value indicate that the line is a great fit to the scatterplot.

I refer to the result of the linear regression analysis as "the linear model."

Making Predictions

Linear regression enables you to predict, and R provides a function that does just that: predict() applies a set of x-values to the linear model and returns the predicted values. Imagine two applicants with Aptitude scores of 85 and 62:

```
predict(FM.reg,data.frame(Aptitude=c(85,62)))
```

The first argument is the linear model, and the second makes a data frame out of the vector of values for the independent variable. Running this function produces these predicted values:

```
        1        2
78.59157 63.55723
```

Chapter **13**

Correlation: The Rise and Fall of Relationships

n Chapter 12, I introduce regression, a tool for summarizing and testing relationships between (and among) variables. In this chapter, I introduce you to the ups and downs of correlation, a regression-related tool for looking at relationships.

I use the example of employee aptitude and performance from Chapter 12 and show how to think about the data in a slightly different way. I also show you how to test hypotheses about relationships and how to use R functions for correlation.

Understanding Correlation

Correlation is a statistical way of looking at a relationship. When two things are correlated, it means that they vary together. *Positive* correlation means that high scores on one are associated with high scores on the other, and that low scores on one are associated with low scores on the other as in the Aptitude-Performance example in Chapter 12.

Negative correlation, on the other hand, means that high scores on the first thing are associated with *low* scores on the second.

Negative correlation also means that low scores on the first are associated with high scores on the second. An example is the correlation between body weight and the time spent on a weight-loss program. If the program is effective, the higher the amount of time spent on the program, the lower the body weight. Also, the lower the amount of time spent on the program, the higher the body weight.

Table 13-1, a repeat of Table 12-1, shows the data for 16 FarMisht consultants.

In keeping with Chapter 12, Aptitude is the x-variable and Performance is the y-variable.

The formula for calculating the correlation between the two is

$$r = \frac{\left[\frac{1}{N-1}\right]\sum(x-\bar{x})(y-\bar{y})}{s_x s_y}$$

The term on the left, r, is called the *correlation coefficient*. It's also called *Pearson's product-moment correlation coefficient*, after its creator, Karl Pearson.

The lower limit of the correlation coefficient is –1.00, and the upper limit is +1.00.

A correlation coefficient of –1.00 represents perfect negative correlation (low x-scores associated with high y-scores, and high x-scores associated with low y-scores). A correlation of +1.00 represents perfect positive correlation (low x-scores associated with low y-scores and high x-scores associated with high y-scores). A correlation of 0.00 means that the two variables are not related.

Applying the formula to the data in Table 13-1,

$$r = \frac{\left[\frac{1}{N-1}\right]\sum(x-\bar{x})(y-\bar{y})}{s_x s_y}$$

$$= \frac{\left[\frac{1}{16-1}\right]\left[\frac{(45-72.81)(56-70.63)+...+(74-72.81)}{(66-70.83)}\right]}{(13.48)(11.25)} = .783$$

TABLE 13-1 Aptitude Scores and Performance Scores for 16 FarMisht Consultants

Consultant	Aptitude	Performance
1	45	56
2	81	74
3	65	56
4	87	81
5	68	75
6	91	84
7	77	68
8	61	52
9	55	57
10	66	82
11	82	73
12	93	90
13	76	67
14	83	79
15	61	70
16	74	66
Mean	72.81	70.63
Variance	181.63	126.65

What, exactly, does this number mean? I'm about to tell you.

Correlation and Regression

Figure 13-1 shows the graph (it's called a "scatterplot") of the 16 employees in Table 13-1. Each point represents the employee's Aptitude score (x) and their Performance score (y). Figure 13-2 also shows the line that "best fits" the points.

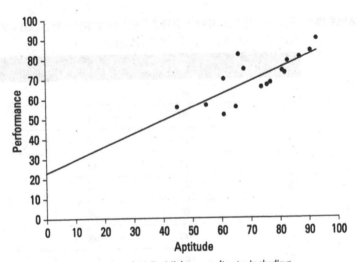

FIGURE 13-1: Scatterplot of 16 FarMisht consultants, including the regression line.

The best-fitting line meets a specific standard: If you draw the distances in the vertical direction between the points and the line, and you square those distances, and then you add those squared distances, the best-fitting line is the one that makes the sum of those squared distances as small as possible. This line is called the *regression line.*

Correlation is closely related to regression. Figure 13-2 focuses on one point in the scatterplot, and on its distance to the regression line and to the mean. (This is a repeat of Figure 12-2.)

Notice the three distances laid out in the figure. The distance labeled (y-y') is the difference between the point and the regression line's prediction for where the point should be. (In Chapter 12, I call that a *residual.*) The distance labeled $(y - \bar{y})$ is the difference between the point and the mean of the y's. The distance labeled $(y' - \bar{y})$ represents the gain in prediction capability that you get from using the regression line to predict the point instead of using the mean to predict the point. It's the difference between the predicted point and the mean of the y's.

Figure 13-2 shows that the three distances are related like this:

$$(y - y') + (y' - \bar{y}) = (y - \bar{y})$$

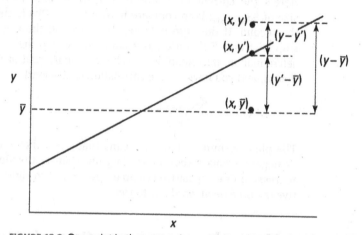

FIGURE 13-2: One point in the scatterplot and its associated distances.

As I point out in Chapter 12, you can square all the residuals and add them up, square all the deviations of the predicted points from the mean and add them up, and square all the deviations of the actual points from the mean and add them up, too.

It turns out that these sums of squares are related in the same way as the deviations I just showed you:

$$SS_{Residual} + SS_{Regression} = SS_{Total}$$

If $SS_{Regression}$ is large in comparison to $SS_{Residual}$, the relationship between the x-variable and the y-variable is a strong one. It means that, throughout the scatterplot, the variability around the regression line is small.

On the other hand, if $SS_{Regression}$ is small in comparison to $SS_{Residual}$, the relationship between the x-variable and the y-variable is weak. In this case, the variability around the regression line is large throughout the scatterplot.

One way to test $SS_{Regression}$ against $SS_{Residual}$ is to divide each by its degrees of freedom (1 for $SS_{Regression}$ and $N-2$ for $SS_{Residual}$) to form variance estimates (also known as mean squares, or MS), and then divide one by the other to calculate an F. If $MS_{Regression}$ is significantly larger than $MS_{Residual}$, you have evidence that the x-y relationship is strong. (See Chapter 12 for details.)

Here's the correlation connection: Another way to assess the size of $SS_{Regression}$ is to compare it with SS_{Total}. Divide the first by the second. If the ratio is large, this tells you the x-y relationship is strong. This ratio has a name. It's called the *coefficient of determination*. Its symbol is r^2. Take the square root of this coefficient, and you have . . . the correlation coefficient!

$$r = \sqrt{r^2} = \pm\sqrt{\frac{SS_{Regression}}{SS_{Total}}}$$

The plus-or-minus sign (±) means that r is either the positive or negative square root, depending on whether the slope of the regression line is positive (slanted upward left to right) or negative (slanted downward left to right).

Testing Hypotheses About Correlation

Like any other kind of hypothesis testing, the idea here is to use a sample statistic to make an inference about a population parameter. In this case, the sample statistic is r, the correlation coefficient. By convention, the population parameter is ρ (rho), the Greek equivalent of r. (Yes, it does look like the letter p, but it really is the Greek equivalent of r.)

Returning once again to the Aptitude-Performance example, you can use the sample r to test hypotheses about the population ρ — the correlation coefficient for all consultants at FarMisht Consulting.

Assuming that you know in advance (before you gather any sample data) that any correlation between Aptitude and Performance should be positive, the hypotheses are

$H_0: \rho \leq 0$

$H_1: \rho > 0$

Set $\alpha = .05$.

The appropriate statistical test is a t-test. The formula is

$$t = \frac{r - \rho}{s_r}$$

This test has $N-2$ df.

For the example, the values in the numerator are set: r is .783 and ρ (in H_0) is 0. What about the denominator? I won't burden you with the details. I'll just tell you that's

$$\sqrt{\frac{1-r^2}{N-2}}$$

With a little algebra, the formula for the t-test simplifies to

$$t=\frac{r\sqrt{N-2}}{\sqrt{1-r^2}}$$

For the example,

$$t=\frac{r\sqrt{N-2}}{\sqrt{1-r^2}}=\frac{.783\sqrt{16-2}}{\sqrt{1-.783^2}}=4.707$$

With df = 14 and α = .05 (one-tailed), the critical value of t is 1.76. Because the calculated value is greater than the critical value, the decision is to reject H_0.

Analyzing Correlation in R

In this section, I work with the FarMisht example. The data frame, FarMisht.frame, holds the data points shown in Table 13-1. Here's how I created it:

```
Aptitude <- c(45, 81, 65, 87, 68, 91, 77, 61, 55,
   66, 82, 93, 76, 83, 61, 74)
Performance <- c(56, 74, 56, 81, 75, 84, 68, 52,
   57, 82, 73, 90, 67, 79, 70, 66)
FarMisht.frame <- data.frame(Aptitude,
   Performance)
```

To calculate a correlation coefficient, and test it at the same time, R provides cor.test(). Here is a one-tailed test (specified by alternative = "greater"):

```
> with(FarMisht.frame, cor.
   test(Aptitude,Performance, alternative =
   "greater"))
```

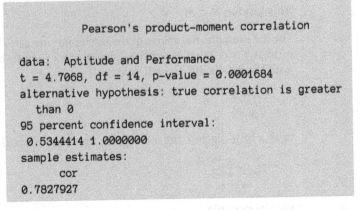

```
                Pearson's product-moment correlation

data:  Aptitude and Performance
t = 4.7068, df = 14, p-value = 0.0001684
alternative hypothesis: true correlation is greater
    than 0
95 percent confidence interval:
 0.5344414 1.0000000
sample estimates:
      cor
0.7827927
```

The high value of *t* (just as I calculated earlier) and its extremely low associated p-value indicate that you reject the null hypothesis. The value of *r* appears at the bottom of the display.

Chapter **14**
Ten Valuable Online Resources

One reason for the rapid rise of R is the supportive R community. It seems that as soon as someone becomes proficient in R, they immediately want to share their knowledge with others — and the web is the place to do it. This chapter points you to some of the helpful web-based resources the R community has created.

R-bloggers

This website (www.r-bloggers.com) comprises the efforts of hundreds of R bloggers and includes news and tutorials. Statistics PhD candidate Tal Galili runs the show. As he says, his objective is to empower R bloggers to empower R users. In addition to the blogs, you'll find links to courses, conferences, and job opportunities.

Posit

The website from which you download RStudio (`https://posit.co`) is a treasure trove of resources for R enthusiasts (and Python enthusiasts, too). You have to pay for many of the resources, but with a little digging around, you can find some helpful freebies, like the "RStudio Cheatsheet."

Quick-R

Wesleyan University professor Rob Kabacoff created this website (`www.statmethods.net`) to introduce people to R and its application to statistical concepts, both introductory and advanced. It has extremely well-written content (and neat graphics).

Stack Overflow

Not limited to R, Stack Overflow (`https://stackoverflow.com`) is a multimillion-member community of programmers dedicated to helping each other. You can search the Q&A base for help with a problem, or you can ask a question. To ask a question, however, you have to be a member (it's free) and log in. The site also provides links to jobs, documentation, and more.

R Manuals

If you want to go directly to the source, visit the R manuals page at `https://cran.r-project.org/manuals.html`. That's where you'll find links to the *R Language Definition* and other documentation.

R Documentation

For links to even more R documentation, try `www.r-project.org/other-docs.html`.

RDocumentation

Wait, didn't I just use this title? Yes, well, the Canadian Football League once had a team named the Rough Riders and another named the Roughriders. It's something like that.

The RDocumentation page at https://rdocumentation.org is quite a bit different from the web page in the previous section. This one doesn't link to manuals and other documents. Instead, this website enables you to search for R packages and functions that suit your needs.

How many packages are available? More than 27,000!

YOU CANanalytics

The brainchild of Roopham Upadhyay, the YOU CANanalytics website (https://ucanalytics.com/blogs) provides a number of helpful blogs and case studies.

The following page enables you to download classic R books as PDFs: http://ucanalytics.com/blogs/learn-r-12-books-and-online-resources. Some of the titles are at the introductory level, some are advanced, and all of them are free!

TIP

A book in PDF form is a very long document. If you're reading it on a tablet, it's more user-friendly to turn the PDF file into an e-book. To do this, upload the PDF into an e-reader like Google Play Books, and — voilà! — your PDF becomes an e-book.

Geocomputation with R

You may want to expand your R skill set into the fascinating area of geographic data analysis. This free online book by Robin Lovelace, Jakub Nowosad, and Jannes Muenchow enables you to do just that. You'll find it at https://r.geocompx.org.

The R Journal

I saved this one for last, because it's at an advanced level. Like academic publications, The *R Journal* is refereed — experts in the field decide whether a submitted article is worthy of publication. Take a look at the articles at https://journal.r-project.org, and you'll see what's in store for you when you become one of those experts!

Index

Symbols

== (double equal-sign), 32
%% (mod operator), 34
$ sign, 52–53

A

a priori tests, 136–137
abs( ) function, 106, 118
absolute zero, 6
alpha, 100
alternative hypothesis, 8–9, 100
analysis of variance (ANOVA)
    about, 43, 134–136
    in R, 136–143
aov( ) function, 43, 134
arguments, 20
assignment operator, 16
asymptotic curve, 84
attach( ) function, 53
attributes, 81

B

bell curve
    about, 81
    probability density (f(x)), 82
    x, 82
beta, 100
bimodal, 55

C

c( ) function, 20, 24
cat( ) function, 106, 118
categorical variables, 28
CDF (cumulative density function), 85–86

central limit theorem
    about, 91–93
    applying, 114
    simulating, 91–93
central tendency
    about, 49
    mean, 49–51
    mean( ), 51–53
    median, 53–55
    median( ), 54–55
    mode, 55
    mode( ), 55
character vector, 21
coefficient of determination, 166
comments, 23
comparison coefficients, 137
components, 24
Comprehensive R Archive Network (CRAN), 11, 40
concatenate, 16
conditional probability, 7
conditions, 64–65
confidence limits
    about, 93
    finding for a mean, 93–96
constant, 5
continuation prompt, 23
contrasts, 136–140
correlation
    about, 161–163
    hypothesis testing about, 166–167
    regression and, 163–166
correlation coefficient, 162
cor.test( ) function, 167–168
CRAN (Comprehensive R Archive Network), 11, 40
CSV files, 45–46

About the Author

Joseph Schmuller is a veteran of academia and the corporate world. He is the author of numerous books on computing, including the three editions of *Teach Yourself UML in 24 Hours* (SAMS), the five editions of *Statistical Analysis with Excel For Dummies* (Wiley), and *R All-in-One For Dummies* (Wiley). His books have been translated into ten languages and his LinkedIn Learning courses have been taken by more than 100,000 learners worldwide.

He is a former member of the American Statistical Association, and he has taught statistics at the undergraduate and graduate levels. He holds a BS from Brooklyn College, an MA from the University of Missouri-Kansas City, and a PhD from the University of Wisconsin, all in psychology. He and his family live in Jacksonville, Florida, where he works on the AI Automation Development Team at Availity.

Dedication

For my friends and colleagues at Availity, who inspire me every day.

Author's Acknowledgments

Although I've written quite a few *For Dummies* titles, this book is a departure for me. Distilling a world of complex ideas into just the essentials is a bigger challenge than it sounds — and it sounds pretty challenging.

Happily, the Wiley team was there to help. Editor Elizabeth Kuball had the unenviable task of reining in my prose; my thanks to her for her guidance and her patience. Once again, I got to work with the great Guy Hart-Davis, who served as technical editor. "The great Guy" seems like an understatement for such a great guy. He always goes above and beyond to make sure a book's code and technical aspects are correct, and I truly appreciate him. Executive editor Lindsay Berg came up with the idea of an *Essentials* series within the *For Dummies* framework. I'm grateful that she invited me to be part of it. Many thanks to my longtime agent and friend David Fugate of Launchbooks.com for representing me in this project.

My mentors in statistics in college and graduate school shaped my knowledge and my thinking and, thus, influenced this book: Mitch Grossberg (Brooklyn College); the late Al Hillix, Jerry Sheridan, the late Mort Goldman, and the late Larry Simkins (University of Missouri–Kansas City); and Cliff Gillman and the late John Theios (University of Wisconsin–Madison). I hope my books are an appropriate testament to my mentors who have passed on.

As always, my thanks to Katherine for her inspiration, her patience, her support, and most of all, for her love.

Publisher's Acknowledgments

Executive Editor: Lindsay Berg
Editor: Elizabeth Kuball
Technical Editor: Guy Hart-Davis

Production Editor: Tamilmani Varadharaj
Cover Design and Image: Wiley